The
Timid
Marine

The
Timid
Marine

◆

Surrender to Combat Fatigue

Joseph Lanciotti

iUniverse, Inc.

New York Lincoln Shanghai

The Timid Marine
Surrender to Combat Fatigue

iUniverse books may be ordered through booksellers or by contacting:

iUniverse
2021 Pine Lake Road, Suite 100
Lincoln, NE 68512
www.iuniverse.com
1-800-Authors (1-800-288-4677)

The names of characters are fictitious. Some names have been changed to protect the privacy of survivors.

ISBN-13: 978-0-595-34866-4 (pbk)
ISBN-13: 978-0-595-79586-4 (ebk)
ISBN-10: 0-595-34866-1 (pbk)
ISBN-10: 0-595-79586-2 (ebk)

Printed in the United States of America

For Vivian
And you who live
because I survived.

Contents

Acknowledgement

To Joanne and Doug Emery for reading the drafts and making critical improvements. As always, their comments and suggestions pointed me to a more professional and honest direction. The editor at iUniverse for encouraging words, and visualizing the final form.

Introduction

My discharge papers read, "Participated in action against the enemy on Okinawa, Ryukyo Islands, April 1, 1945, June 30, 1945. Participated in the occupation of China Oct. 25, 1945, Aug. 19, 1946. Weapon qualification rifle, sharpshooter, and bayonet. Character of service, EXCELLENT."

There was so much more. Let me tell you what happened. I am one of millions of little people who are born in this world and have dreams of becoming something more than the world has planned for them to be. As a young boy I dreamt of leaving my small town where my family lived very close to poverty, and the movies fueled my brain with ideas and day dreams I waited to happen.

Then it happened, the opportunity to leave my old town, to travel and to be recognized as somebody. It was World War II, the only war experience I would have that was forever a part of American history.

War to many is confused with the Sunday football game where the combatants bruise and bloody each other for the entertainment of thousands of spectators. Much of the football terminology is transferred to the war experience. *The Red Badge Of Courage*, by Stephen Crane, who had never been in a war, was based, according to him, on his knowledge of football. People say this book is the definitive book on war. I don't think so.

If all that is required to describe war is a string of words using football terminology and a search for courage, then any literate person could do it. The truth is that no one, especially one who has not been in a war, can really describe what occurs on a battle field adequately, to convey its utter waste and horror. Even those who witnessed it personally can't use the words to exactly describe it as it was. They can only try, and fail.

A war consists of thousands of engagements, large and small, between men who are told by their governments that their participation in it is necessary and critical. Each side enlists the backing of God, and each side is certain that it is in the right. The tapestry of war is a large and intricate. One man is a very small thread lost in its complexity.

We may read thousands of books about what a war was from those who had touched it briefly during moments of confusion and fear. Each will use the words horror, terror and pain. They will create graphic sentences to recount experiences with the greatest impact, but will always fall short of the mark of attaining the truth. But if you shared a foxhole during combat for one night, words would not be necessary to explain anything to you..

War is a frightful and demeaning experience that quickly reduces a man or woman to a breaking point. Civilized men and even poets become calloused and brutalized during their exposure in it. With all its madness, pain, fear and constant degrading of the human spirit, it distorts reality and humanity, and creates a hellish other-world that is beyond definitive description. Words alone cannot convey the insanity of it. One must be immersed in the blood, stench, fear and agony of it until he is almost insane, to approach understanding. However, I intend to grab you by the scruff of your neck and stick your nose into the reality of it.

During World War II hundreds of thousands of men were rejected for psychological reasons that indicated that they would not endure combat. Of the millions who were accepted, more than 1,393,000 were treated for combat fatigue. Of all ground combat troops, 37 percent were discharged for psychiatric reasons.

During the war millions of service men were lucky to never see combat to test their courage. More than ten men were required in the rear areas to keep one man at the front. And those who had to face the enemy deserted by the thousands when they found the opportunity.

Of these thousands, the United States executed only one man for desertion and combat fatigue during World War II. He was the first to be executed by the government since the Civil War. He was tied to a post and killed by a firing squad comprised of his buddies. I, and hundreds of thousands of combat fatigued veterans could sympathize with Eddie Slovik, that frightened soldier.

I was a very frightened and timid Marine.

1

War Games, Parris Island

President Truman says Marines have propaganda machine equal to Stalin's. 1950 NY Times
 Three Recruits drown while training at Parris Island. 1952 NY Times.
 Recruit maltreatment persisting in Marines despite official ban. 1969 NY Times.
 Recruit dies in training at Parris Island. 2005 NY Times.

December 1941

Night seemed to fall earlier and colder that winter in America but the Adventures of Jack Armstrong, The Shadow and The Green Hornet on the radio kept millions of young boys entertained, and made time pass more quickly. On Sunday nights the country listened to comedy shows like Fibber Magee and Molly, Fred Allen and Jack Benny. The world needed some laughter while so many were dying.

The news was full of places where people were being killed and armies were moving. Millions of us were caught up in the rolling wave of history that was taking us along a terrible ride that would change us forever, if we survived. The sad, slow days of the war in Europe would stun us for years. The toll was so horrible that they were not accepted as factual by many. Concentration camps brought horrors never before imagined and some people chose to disbelieve the facts rather than accept the truth of such repugnant insanity. But to us these were only news stories on the radio or in the papers which we did not read as kids.

I was setting up pins for Pop Mahon's second game in Lodi, New Jersey. He had scored two thirty in the first and he was not pleased with that. It was around the second or third frame when the small, St. Francis Church bowling alley became ominously quiet that Sunday afternoon. The hum of the bowling balls rolling down the waxed lanes, the crack of the balls against the wooden pins and the slam of the pins against the side of the pin pit had all stopped.

The pin setters in the other pits looked at each other and then over at me with a puzzled look. I could not provide any information to change their expression.

Pop was up but did not take his ball from the rack. He was talking to some of the older guys about something and they turned the radio louder. Pop then waved the pin boys up to the front bowling alley and we all ran to see what was going on.

Pop was the manager and we all liked him. He must have been in his fifties and a great bowler. He paid us five cents a game for setting pins on Sunday afternoons and our gang of kids loved spending time there to make a few bucks and to bowl for free.

Someone on the radio was talking excitedly about the Japanese bombing Pearl Harbor in the Hawaiian Islands, that it was a sneak attack and that many Americans were dead.

I don't think that even Pop knew where Pearl Harbor was, although the Hawaiian Islands were familiar from the movies. Our gang of teenage pin boys, still in high school, did not understand what was happening but felt that it was important by the way the older guys were talking and reacting to the radio news.

Some of the older guys looked like ghosts with the blood drained from their faces and I didn't realize until years later what this had meant to them. They had just finished a year of required military duty and getting ready to put some civilian dreams into reality, and now they were confronted with a war that would take another three years or more from their lives, if not their lives completely.

A couple of Civilian Conservation Corps guys who were in their green uniforms knew that their days in the woods chopping trees for Uncle Sam were about over. They would be changing their green CCC uniforms for one of the military styles. I, and my friends did not know how this news would impact on us at our age. We felt protected by our youth. Eighteen was the enlistment age for the draft and the war would not last two or three years in our minds. At fifteen, three years was a century away.

That important, magical event some of us were hoping for that would change our boring lives had come without warning. Daily events continued to push us along with the history of the time as we continued living our high school days. Those who had served their mandatory year were recalled, and the draft machinery would be slowly demanding more men as the country continued to fight a World War which it had supposedly sought to avoid.

That Christmas of 1941 saw most of us as poor as we had ever been. My father, had been to a veteran hospital in Staten Island for a hernia operation paid by the government and was returning on Christmas Eve. It was a cold night and my younger brother and I had little to eat, a few sausages, potatoes and bread. Our two room apartment was heated by a pot belly kerosene stove burning in the middle of the kitchen. I was fifteen and my brother thirteen. Our mother had deserted the family and the old man was in a hospital for a operation.

During the night the snow began to come down and slowly began to build. It was beautiful to see. I always liked the snow. Then out of the night a figure appeared on the front porch of our rented rooms which was on the first floor of an old farm house that had been remodeled into several apartments. It was my father returning from the hospital. He had walked from the bus stop a good distance away. Years later I realized that he must have been in pain so soon after surgery and walking the long distance in the snow. He did not complain.

As my father entered the house, and I looked out of the window into the snow-filled yard, the radio commentator was talking about thousands of people who were dying in concentration camps. Men, women and children were dying throughout the world because of the war. Britain was being bombed, Europe and Russian and the entire world was in turmoil. I understood only as much as my age and small intelligence permitted, which was very little.

The war was still young for the country's teenagers who were fated to meet in a few years for an adventure they could never have imagined. The Hollywood propaganda machine was already planning movies to excite young boys to join the military.

In 1941 Dan Kruplowski in Conshohocken, Pennsylvania was playing great football in high school, James Long in Philadelphia, had a great time keeping up with all his girl friends at the many dances he attended; Louie LaForse in Hooksett, New Hampshire was enjoying the best hunting he had ever experienced, and I, in Lodi, New Jersey had dropped out of high school and decided to become a poet.

We had several things in common, we were about the same age, relatively poor, and our time to save the world had come. My father was an immigrant soldier who bought his citizenship serving in World War I and told me stories of how his generation saved the world, now it was our turn in World War II. Now it was my generation's turn.

In their various locations the local dignitaries gathered on that indoctrination day, May 4, 1944, to give the new heroes a send off. All of us just a few days ago were still delivering newspapers, playing football and listening to the Andrew Sisters singing, *The Boogie, Woggie Bugle Boy of Company B, Don't Sit Under The Apple Tree,* and other songs that identified that time.

The mayor and other officials, made patriotic speeches containing the usual words, duty, country, God, bravery, and so on. The American Legion Auxiliary women gave out cigarettes, coffee and doughnuts and little pouches of stuff that was mostly useless but you felt good getting something free. The women smiled and were proud of their participation in the war effort. That was as close as they would get to the war. They all meant well.

My old elementary school principal, Mrs. Sarah Mercer from Lodi was there. She was tall, white haired and wore steel rimmed spectacles and an expensive, blue cloth coat with a fake fur collar. It must have cost at least thirty five dollars. You knew she was someone important just by her coat. I always felt that she was as rich person.

She had gold bridge work and fillings in some of her teeth and you could see them gleam when she smiled big, and the sun hit them. She wore her hair short and I always thought she looked like George Washington, just like the copy of Stuart's painting hanging on the Wilson School wall.

As principal of the Wilson School she was a big shot, a figure of authority to us kids, and I felt important that she was there to see me off to fight for the country. I knew it was an important day because she was there and I was proud to be in her company almost as an equal now. Her high pitched voice called us "her boys" with the same authority that only a few years ago intimidated us in the school yard.

It was about the same in the other towns we came from. The entire country sort of fell into line on these ceremonies sending their boys off to war. The same level of celebrities gathered and said the same words, and the volunteer ladies smiled and handed out small gifts.

There, too, were our families, Polish, Jews, Irish, Italian, and French-Canadian, all represented. The songs of Bing Crosby, the big bands on the radio, all that music sending us off. Bing's voice had become a part of our culture. I still remember his voice, so familiar, he was singing as I left my apartment, "a mule is an animal with long funny ears and laughs at everything he hears,...do you want to grow up to be a mule?...So you better go to school." If you were living at that time you knew that song.

This was an odd song for me to remember for one of the most important days of my life, I thought, but life's funny that way about what you remember and forget. Anyway, the advice was too late for me, I had dropped out of school two years ago.

Parents, friends and local dignitaries smiled sadly as the buses pulled up to take us away. They had a good idea of where we would be going. Some fathers and mothers and sisters and brothers, uncles and aunts came. My best friend, Billy, was there to see me off. He was a year younger than I. Our childhood and adolescent friendship ended on that day.

We, newly drafted heroes, boarded the buses. We waved back at the spectators, the families, and my friend Billy seemed so serious and sad. I had said good-bye to my father at home, and my kid brother had gone to school without saying anything. We were that way with each other despite a deep, silent love we shared.

As the bus pulled away I saw the figure of this shy little man with a bald head. It was my father. He was ashamed to be in the crowd and waved at me from a distance. He had tears in his eyes. He had followed me after I left the house, and walked behind me all the way to ceremony. He knew where I was traveling. Seeing him, I began to cry, and the bus pulled away.

The people at the ceremony all returned home to continue their lives, and we began our long journey. That journey, two and a half years in time for those who returned, would place a brand in our hearts forever. We would remember as long as we lived how our families looked at us that day. Fathers were so grim, and mothers and sisters had to be consoled for days, years, and sometimes, for lifetimes, if their loved ones did not return.

Those of us who had volunteered to join the Marine Corps were sworn in at our various state enlistment centers where we were told the importance of our oath of allegiance to the country and the Marines. We were reminded that we volunteered by our own choice and were not drafted like the other services. In other words, we had asked for it. We were in for the duration of the war, however long that would be. There was no cut off time for this war, if they needed you, you would be there to the end.

We, new Marine recruits, were boarded on a train heading for Parris Island, South Carolina. As it came down from New England, into the New York, Newark and Philadelphia it picked us up on a prearranged schedule that the government had arranged with the railroad.

It was the first train ride that I could remember well. The other being the one as an infant, which was mostly a haze of bodily functions and odors. This was recalled when the brain reaches far back into stored memories, and you wonder why.

The train was old and rusty, fading green and the windows were painted black because of the war. It strained and complained like any old piece of machinery whose parts did not fit tightly anymore and grease alone could not remedy. Riding with open windows during the day permitted cinders from the engines to fly back into the compartments and coated us with grit and grime. The seats were unpadded and the compartments cramped. I felt that I was on the greatest, most wonderful adventure of my life. I had graduated from living vicariously through the movies and books all my short life to finally doing something on my own, something original and important.

The train stopped in Washington, D.C. and we were ordered off for a little exercise before continuing the journey. We were an odd bunch of young men and boys, mostly boys, with clothing clashing in color and style, a variety of hair-cuts, all in stages of disarray. We were comical to look at, unruly, undisciplined, awkward and clumsy.

We were quickly recognized by uniformed Marines who were at the train station on their way to various parts of the country for liberty or duty. They had completed their Boot Camp training which we were headed for and found the sight of us sadly comical and perhaps familiar, having been in the same position themselves only several weeks before.

"You'll be s-o-r-r-y?", came a jeering voice over the din of the station and then another voice repeating the same warning., "You'll be s-o-r-r-y!"

We knew the warning was aimed at us.

From that time onward, whenever a group of Marines was entering a questionable or difficult situation a voice from somewhere would call out, and remind them of the first time they heard those taunting words.

"You'll be s-o-r-r-y," became a standard warning that we all recognized. We knew that warning sentence, called out in jest, conveyed the coming of a dire condition.

We arrived in Parris Island in the dark but the bus was still hot from the sun that beat down on it all day. We accused the Corps of parking the bus in the sun purposely, and realized later it was a typical Marine Corps tactic.

A man who said he was our Drill Instructor shouted at us to get on the bus and keep quite. He told us that we were not Marines yet and he was going to make us Marines even if it killed him. Because we arrived on the Island late he had little time to give us a long lecture and got down to the basics. We were to obey everything he told us to do. Everything. We would soon find out that he meant everything. Then he told us that Parris island was surrounded by several swift running rivers and creeks and that if we tried to escape we would either drown or be eaten by sharks. Then he left.

He would be known as our DI, and we would see him early the next morning.

The bus driver took us to a large building where we were issued uniforms and underwear that seemed too large for us and designed to make us look more foolish than we were. Little by little we would be stripped of all the signs that made us individuals, civilians, free men, and slowly they would punish us into being Marines.

All the issued gear was packed into a sea bag which we had never seen before and did not know how to use properly. The narrow, canvas bag was about two feet in diameter and three feet high. Clothing had to be folded precisely and carefully to fit into the bag and not be overly wrinkled when removed. It would take many days to learn the technique but for the first night we just stuffed everything in without care.

When we lay our weary bodies down on our cots that night most of us did not take long to fall asleep. Those who were too frightened by the ordeal, sobbed quietly in the dark before leaving consciousness.

One or two had to relieve their tension by masturbating. If the masturbator was in the upper bunk he was detected more quickly by the creaking than if he were in the lower. The sound of the creaking bunk was amplified in the dark, quiet room and several voices would yell out, "knock it off you pervert." Those still awake snickered.

The night ended before beginning. Our heads touched the pillows one minute and then a loud bugle was blaring and Drill Instructors were stamping around the barracks calling everyone names. Our refuge in sleep had been brief.

"Shit heads, shit birds, knuckle heads, masturbators, civilian, mommy boys."

"Get dressed and fall out in ten minutes."

My transition from a no-schedule teenager to this atmosphere was startling. My companions voiced the same stunned disbelief as to what was happening to us.

Off we marched to the first chow line of our Marine experience. The morning was still cool because the sun had not come up. It burned just below the rim of the horizon sending a weak light into the sky of a new day that would be hot and humid before it was done.

"Wun up reep, wun up reep, wun up your lelf," the DI shouted once we fell in on his command. This strange cadence at first was difficult to understand but soon became a compelling and insistent song we obeyed..

When we entered the chow hall, the veterans of two weeks Boot Camp recognized our platoon as new recruits and you could sense their feeling of superiority by their snickering.

As the trays were held out at the chow line they were filled quickly and haphazardly. Dessert mixed with pork chops and potatoes, but it was good food and warm. We ate voraciously, and I, better than ever before in my life. I especially was awed by the abundance of cold milk in large metal pitchers, the variety of fruit and pies and pastries. My breakfast at home would have been a jelly dough-nut and coffee.

Within twenty minutes chow was over and we fell into ranks for another fast march at double time. We never were told where we were going but always seemed to be going there urgently under double time.

We were at the barber shop where our civilian hair styles fell to the floor in a common mound, and we were reduced to one style. Bald. In less than a minute each man was shorn clean, and the red, blond, brown, and black locks slid off the bald domes creating a thick, multi-colored mat on the barber's floor.

Now bald, wearing clothing that was ill fitting, and with a dazed look on our faces, we continued our transformation. Stripped of all past identification includ-ing a name, we were identified by the DI as shit bird, shit head, Boot, and an assortment of other names, but not our own.

Never were we called Marine. A given number that identified us would be in our minds until the day we died. (I was, am, and will be 971571 in the records of the Corps.) That number became our identification and would be placed on our dog tags along with our civilian name, religion, P, C, or J. and blood type, A, B or O. And oh yes, USMCR.

The last designation was to remind you that you were not fully a member of the USMC. The R designated you as a Reserve, a step below the elite who were professionals who were USMC. The reserves were only in for the duration of the war while the professionals were in forever. The professionals were proud of the distinction.

One dog tag would be taken by the graves registration personnel when we were killed in action, if could be found, leaving the other in the grave to intro-duce us to God.

During long and intensive days we were drilled day and sometimes night, with the singsong cadence of the Drill Instructor humming in our ears. "Wun up reep wun up your lelf. Wun reep, wun up your lelf." Over and over. "One up three. One up your left. One up three, one up your left. Your left right left. Wun up reep, wun up your lelf."

Each cadence caller added his own version to the call. Each recruit marched with the beat and sound of it on the parade field, marching to chow, marching anywhere. "One, up three, one up your left, or wan hup reep one up yo llef."

The purpose, of course, was to get us to march in unison, learn to obey orders and to present a military appearance. Within a few days most had the idea down basically and then we were introduced to our rifle, which added a new dimension to the marching drill.

The training continued with this important information by the Drill Instructor as he handed us our rifles.

"You hold in your hands the reason the country is paying for your food and shelter and gives you good, American dollars every month to buy cigarettes, beer and candy."

We would learn how to take the rifle apart and then put it back together again. Some would do this blindfolded with considerable pride. We would polish and oil every part of it and learn about how wonderfully it could kill.

"You are holding in your hands the most important friend you will ever have in your life," the DI continued his sermon to the platoon.

"This is your caliber .30 M1 Garand rifle. It is a gas operated, semiautomatic weapon. It is 43.6 inches long, weights 9 pounds, 8 ounces unloaded. It is clip fed with eight rounds of .30-06 caliber ammunition. The clip is ejected automatically after the last round is fired. Muzzle velocity 2800 feet per second. Effective range, 440 yards,"

It was like learning the Star Spangled Banner in grade school. You repeated the words not knowing what they meant or even how to pronounce them correctly.

"You will love this rifle and you will sleep with it in combat like it was your best girl friend. You will never drop it, you will keep it as clean, no, cleaner, than you keep your little gun between your legs," The DI continued.

"Remember, between your legs is your gun and this is your rifle. One is for killing and the other for fun."

Some snickered but the look on the DI's face soon made the snickers fade. The DI did not make an issue of the snickering because he had been through that phase with other platoons. He would take his revenge in due time.

When an unfortunate Boot referred to his rifle as his "gun" several days later the DI erupted.

"What did I tell you this weapon was called?"

"Rifle, Sir"

"Well, why did you call it your gun?"

"Do you know where your gun is Boot?"

"Yes Sir," the Boot answered.

"Well, I want you to go around the barracks shouting to everyone you see what you've learned."

"Take your rifle and show it to everyone and say 'this is my rifle' and then hold your crotch and say 'this is my gun'", he ordered.

"Then tell them which is for killing and which is for fun."

The Boot did as instructed, going from Marine to Marine showing his rifle and saying, "this is my rifle," and then holding his crotch saying, "this is my gun".

"One for killing and the other for fun."

He continued like the Ancient Mariner to tell his woeful story until ordered to stop, and anyone who found it humorous did not dare show it to the Drill Instructor. Only when away from his authority would they laugh at the punished Boot. Their laughter was not genuine, however, because they knew they too could make an error and be similarly humiliated.

Our M1 rifles soon became part of our long drills. Shoulder arms, present arms, left shoulder arms, right shoulder arms, inspection arms. At times when a Boot could not get the knack of rifle drill the Drill Instructor would hover over him shouting and sneering the commands.

I had tears in my eyes when the command to left shoulder from right shoulder arms confused me so much that I could not move the rifle properly. One of the older instructors saw my confusion and calmed me down so that I could hear the orders and follow them without fear. Slowly, with a little kindness, no name calling and a little patience the DI taught me. I could see in his eyes that he did not intend to harm me. It was rare act of understanding here.

Words are necessary to first convey information to a group of recruits but there was nothing like experience to imbed information in the human brain. The DI had warned us of the importance of our rifle and he also taught us to obey orders.

"No one ever moves while he is standing at attention. No one moves, understand?"

"Yes sir," the recruits shouted but the Drill Instructor feigned a lack of hearing and said," I can't hear youuuuuu."

And again the recruits replied loudly, "**YES SIR**."

The DI knew that we would not really understand until he taught us a lesson. He knew we believed we understood, but really did not. He would try us again when he was ready.

One long, hard day melted into another all passing with days of the summer of 1944 and our young days were spent in a continuous drills, marches, and learning the ways of the Corps. Little by little, at his leisure, at his best opportunity, the DI would strike out to drive home a lesson he had taught over and over to previous Boot platoons.

To help him teach us the number one commandment of the Corps, "you will obey orders", he chose as his accomplice, the sand gnat.

The sand gnat, culicoides furens. Also called "no-see-ums" are members of a group of insects known as biting midges. Their wings beat over a thousand times per second rendering them almost invisible. The females uses the elongated mandibles in its barbed proboscis to inflict a stinging bite. At the same time a chemical in the saliva prevents blood clotting and permits it to be drawn into the insect as the capillaries bleed. They live in wet sands and thrive on warm temperature and high humidity. On hot, humid and windless days they can attack a man and feast silently so that only the pain of their bites indicate their presence.

It was a hot and humid morning when we fell out for drill. The sand swarmed with invisible sand gnats and they bit into us, and flew up our noses and into our ears as we marched and drilled. Our platoon was standing at attention when the DI noticed a movement in the ranks that offended him. After so many warnings about not moving in the ranks and obeying orders, he knew that some shit head would dare break the first commandment. Someone always did.

A man moved in the rear row. It was a quick, furtive movement chanced by one who knows he is about to commit a mortal sin and did not want to be caught.

The Boot had been enduring the gnat bites but was unable to withstand this particular gnat that seemed to be boring inside his nostril. He reached a hand to stop his tormentor. No one could have seen that quick flick of the hand across his face unless you were a Parris Island Drill Instructor.

"Did I see you move, shit head?" the DI asked with a surprisingly calm and friendly voice to the platoon in general. We were all shit heads and he obviously could be talking to any one of us. But the recruit he was talking to knew that he was being addressed personally, because he knew that he had moved and a cold fear ran down his spine.

He did not answer for two reasons. One reason, he hope that someone else had also moved, and two, he knew not to talk in ranks unless the DI talked to you personally.

Now the soft query was repeated without doubt as to who was being addressed.

"Did you move in ranks while at attention, Boot?"

The DI had moved from the front of the platoon to the rear row and stood in front of the guilty man and was looking into his eyes, a nose length away.

There was a hateful pain on the DI's face and the veins on his neck bulged, and his mouth spat out saliva as he shouted, spraying the recruit's face in small flecks.

"Yes sir," the frighten man said.

Again, the DI pretended not to hear.

"I can't hear **Youuuuuuu**." the DI shouted into the sad face.

"**YES SIR**," the Boot answered with a shout that could be heard several platoons away.

"Why did you move?," the DI asked.

"A gnat was biting me sir."

"Don't you like gnats?"

"No sir."

"Did you kill the gnat?'"

"Yes Sir".

"Don't you know that gnats on this island are government property and don't belong to you? Why did you kill it?"

The recruit was at a lost for an answer. He kept silent and so did the DI, letting the silence add to the torment. We all knew the silence would not last and the DI would concoct a painful punishment for this lack of obedience.

"Murderer, shit head, murderer, that's what you are, you killed that gnat in cold blood. All it wanted to do was eat a little. You were at attention and you moved to kill it."

The DI stated his case, and his verdict, now came the judgment.

"We will have a funeral for this gnat," he said without a smile.

The recruit kept silent about this astounding proposal, and could not imagine what was to follow.

"Do you hear me Boot?"

"**Yes Sir.**"

"Will we give the poor gnat a funeral?"

"**Yes Sir.**"

This drama continued while the platoon was still at attention and the gnats continued to swarm silently and invisibly, biting at will.

We were thinking, "How the hell are you going to give a funeral for a gnat that you can't see in the first place?"

The DI knew how.

"Okay shit heads"—we were told, "we're going to have a funeral for the gnat this shit head killed. Gnats are the property of the United States government and will not be killed by a Boot while he is at attention."

The DI ordered the platoon to fall out and look for the murdered gnat. The gnat, as everyone knew, could not be seen, so how could it be found? We did not dare ask this question.

"Get on you hands and knees and look for the gnat," he told our platoon of about seventy five men who immediately obeyed and began looking for the invisible gnat.

After a half hour crawling around pretending to look for the gnat on the parade ground and sand, without success, of course, we were marched away leaving the guilty recruit looking for the gnat.

The DI marched us down the parade ground once more. Wun up reep, reep up your lelf. One, up, three, one up, your left. We marched gracefully in unison, our boots echoing the cadence commands across the parade ground.

The gnat killer heard the DI's voice fading in the distance as he continued searching for something he could not see. He dared not to stop, because he was "ordered" not to.

Many in the platoon resented the errant Boot for killing the gnat, for moving in ranks, for disobeying orders. That was part of the strategy. The error of one affected all. Disobeying orders was not to be accepted because it affects everyone.

We had all suffered the humility of looking for a gnat for a ridiculous funeral.

As one DI shouted the cadence from the head of the platoon, another circled in the rear from left to right, on the alert for any errors, any misstep, any mistake that would bring him swooping down on the perpetrator screaming into his ear the error he had made.

At times a third DI circled and watched for infractions. The seventy five man platoon marching to the cadence of the DI was transferred into one obedient entity, a single thing comprised of bodies and brains, but now silent and obedient.

An hour later the cadence of wun up reep, reep up your lelf returned to the hearing range of the weary man still looking for the gnat. In his desperation to produce the gnat, he had a collected a handful of insects to offer the DI for his appraisal. He knew he had not found the gnat. There was no gnat to be found. He hoped to please the DI with his insect collection. He expected some sort of recognition for that. He waited for the DI's reaction.

The DI pretended to take an insect from the man's hand without indicating what it was.

"Okay, now we need a coffin. Go find a match box," he said.

In a short time the recruit found a wooden matchbox about one inch by two inches in size which were plentiful around the area. The DI 'placed' the invisible gnat into the match box.

"We are going to have a burial detail for this gnat," he said.

We were marched off to a sandy area as the guilty man followed carrying the 'coffin'. When we reached the sandy burial ground, the DI ordered the us to stand at attention while the one man burying detail scooped up sand deep enough to bury a large dog. Finally he was told to stop and bury the gnat, stand at attention, and salute.

We were all our brothers keepers in the Corps. Each man was given the tacit duty to keep his comrade under surveillance for better or for worse. This made it easier for two DIs to control, humiliate and train a 70 to 80 man platoon. You took care of your buddy, and made sure he was not harmed, but you also made sure he did not foul up. We knew if he did, we all would suffered the punishment.

Supposedly this buddy system would carry over into combat when we were to protect each other and save our own lives.

All the days of summer in that year became a series of drills, marches, lectures about war games. At his leisure, the DI would devise a new war game to hammer home a lesson. We were constantly apprehensive as to what the next move would be, unless we were asleep.

We were sound asleep when the familiar snarl of the DI's voice tore us from our brief nightly escape.

"Fall Out!", he shouted early that morning while banging his baton inside an empty metal trash can causing a harsh and unnecessary noise so early in the day. He had another game to play.

All the Drill Instructors called their platoons out and lined them up at attention before a platform that was built on the edge of the parade ground. On the platform was a major and several other officers with ranks of captain and lieutenants.

The major spoke.

"Men," he said. He was an officer and would never call you Marine until you had finished Boot Camp, but he would not call you Boot or shit head either like the DI's did. Officers were above name calling and profanity when addressing Boots.

"In your training here you will learn some of the most important lessons of being a Marine."

"At times you will give everything you've got, and when you have given that, you will be ordered to give more."

Then he added some other words about the men who had gone before us to fight in distant places with honor, and then ordered the Drill Instructors to take over. The Drill Instructors marched their platoons off away from each other, and then our DI had us fall out and sit on the hot, black pavement.

"You feel how hard and hot this deck is", he said, "Well by the end of this day you will be able lay here and it will feel like a feather bed."

He then ordered us to fall in and began marching us back and forth in quick step across black pavement of the parade ground that stretched into the horizon. Looking down the long black stretch of asphalt you could see the shimmering mirages of glassy pools that glared on the surface and the waves of heat rising.

"One up reep, one up reep," the DIs called their cadence to keep us marching without pause. There were three instructors on duty today and they took turns calling the cadence. We wore green fatigue uniforms with long sleeves and long pant legs. From a distance the platoons of men with legs moving in unison looked like large caterpillars crawling along the ground.

The instructors wore short sleeve khaki shirts, thin khaki pants, and pith helmets to protect them from the punishing sun. Some carried batons which they occasionally rapped on heads and shins of those who made mistakes. They moved up and down with the marching men but preserved their energy by sharing the duty. One could rest as the platoon returned and he would take over the cadence.

"One up reep, one up your lelf. Your left right your left."

The repeated chant hummed in our ears and coaxed us to automatically continue its bidding. We knew they were testing our endurance, and we were determined to take all the punishment they could dish out without quarter as players did on the football field. We wanted to show them we could take it, and that was exactly what they wanted us to do. It was a game.

After several hours of marching you saw the green uniforms in front of you turn black with sweat, and stained white with human salt where the sweat had dried around the edges. You could see rivulets of sweat ran down the necks of the men in front of you and their pant legs beginning to darken with moisture.

One man fell when he ran out of salt. The DI shouted for us to, "march over him, kick him out of the way." making us think about his sanity. Another fell and another. The endless "reep, reep, reep" continued, and you wondered when you would pass out like others along the line.

Our legs were numbed by fatigue and the heat of the black asphalt burned into the soles of our boots. The leather creases cut into our toes and heels where the bending foot scrapped over and over and created a burning, painful blister that filled with water and salt, and then breaks, leaving the raw flesh exposed to the rub of wet socks and tough leather.

After that we were ordered to fall out and rest.

We fell to the hot parade ground where the tar patches in places were melting like soft licorice. Platoons of men in green uniforms, sopping wet from their own sweat sprawled on the ground. Clouds of cigarette smoke fill the air as we took this small pleasure when the DI said, "the smoking lamp is lit."

Then the words of the Marine Major returned and never would leave your brain, "you will be asked to do more than you believed possible to do."

The DI was right too. The hard parade ground felt like a "feather mattress" as we lay on it exhausted.

After a few minutes of rest, the command of the Drill Instructor's voice brought us to our feet and we began marching again. This would be that "extra effort" that you never believed you would be able to make but you made it, or fell unconscious trying.

The men who had fallen during this grueling march were not stepped on or kicked over by their buddies as ordered by the DI. We would not do that. If someone did he would suffer a brutal revenge from the others. It was just a mean command by the DI to startle and brutalize us. They knew that men would be passing out and had medical attention ready to take care of them.

Our blistered and burning feet pained us as we marched back to barracks. Whispered profanities passed through the ranks without caution for the DIs, but they were no longer in a punishing mood anyway, and if they heard the complaints they ignored it. There was a special sound to the DI's cadence as he marched us to the barracks. It exposed a pride in his voice which was louder than usual, more lilting and clear.

"One up reep, one up your lelf! Your lelf, your lelf, your right up lelf!"

As much as we resented the pain they caused us that day, we knew that they were proud of our endurance. Despite our hatred of the DI and his humiliating punishments, there was something in us that wanted to please him and be accepted in his eyes and his Marine Corps. We wanted to show him that we were worthy of belonging as much as he. As we marched to the barracks our steps were defiant and smooth despite our pain. Our close order drill was crisp, clean and cocky, relaying to him our message, "shout your fucking head off, you bastard, you couldn't wear us out." War games are only for young men.

That night we cleaned the blood and broken skin from our blistered feet. Broke blisters with scissors to release trapped water and clipped away the peeling skin. Applied the necessary medications, and prepared for tomorrow when we would learn to throw grenades.

During childhood war games, throwing hand grenades was familiar to boys. Perhaps it was only a rock, a tin can or a empty soda bottle, but it was a hand grenade in our minds. Also, after years of throwing various types of balls, we felt comfortable with the heft of a grenade in our mitt.

"You shit birds will have to pay close attention to the training today," the DI warned.

"One mistake and it could be your asses, and more important, my ass too."

"So stay alert, keep your ears open and follow closely what we say. I don't want any grab-assing, or you will be very sorry. I promise you."

"Now fall in," he said. And we did, with a flurry of heavy boots stamping on wooden floors that echoed through the barracks and down the wooden stairs like a rumble of drums. Young feet heal fast.

We marched to the grenade training field at double time to get us awake in the early morning haze not yet steamed into humidity by the low sun. It was another hot day coming again but the early sun was kind. As it rose into the sky it would turn the moisture into steam.

The DI's voice was especially calm and clear. He did not want anything to slip by us. Learning to throw hand grenades was an important lesson and he had only one day to teach it. The next time we would see grenades would be in advance training in New River, North Carolina, if we got to that training, or in combat. In combat, some men found themselves at the front and had never received grenade training.

The DI held a grenade in his hand high over his head like it was some sort of religious relic. He turned to the right and left of the column of boots that stood facing him. A high mound of dirt and grass ran the length of the throwing area. The mound was to protect us from shrapnel when the thrown grenade exploded. On the other side of the mound were several dummy buildings with wooden window cut outs located at various distances and heights. These were our targets.

"Now listen up," the DI said as his eyes raked across or faces.

"This is a live grenade."

He explained the nomenclature of the weapon, weight, fragments, how to pull the pin and release the handle, how it took four to five seconds to detonate after the handle flew off.

The DI explained how fragments of a hand grenade when exploded, rise from the point of explosion in a gradual upward slant.

"Your best bet to survive a grenade explosion near you is to fall flat on the ground no matter how close you are to the explosion."

"Got that?," he shouted to verify our understanding.

His eyes made contact with every face in the group before he continued.

"Don't ever try to out-run an exploding grenade. One of the fragments will get you."

"Got that,?" he tested again.

"Don't ever try to out-run an exploding grenade," he repeated again.

The grenade he held in his hand was pale green, and serrated into fragments that would break loose and fly slanting upward on explosion. It had a pin with a large, circular ring that held a silver, spoon-like handle to the main body. It looks like a small pineapple, some said.

"We will now pass out practice grenades for you to learn how to pull the pin, release the handle, and throw at the target. Remember the live grenade explodes in four to five seconds. Get rid of it fast."

Before distributing practice grenades, the DI pulled the pin on the grenade he held in his hand and pretended to accidentally drop it. The primer powder of the grenade was smoking. (The primer charge is what ignites the main charge and explodes the fragments.) There was a moment of panic when we saw the DI's grenade fall to the ground at our feet, and some began to run.

A few stopped in our tracks remembering what the DI had said about grenade fragments, and fell to the ground to protect ourselves, others just kept running.

The main powder charge in the DI's grenade had been removed and it was a harmless grenade.

The primer just hissed some smoke and then stopped after an few seconds.

It was a scary lesson. First the fear of being killed by the dropped grenade commanded us to run and try to escape it. Then the DI's instructions were recalled by most of us and we fell to the ground.

The men who had run far away from the grenade, sheepishly returned to our training area where they were jeered. We who had fallen close to the grenade as instructed smiled smugly for our good judgment and recalling the DI's advice.

When we had all settled down the DI had us throw a few dummy grenades at the dummy targets. He was not going to trust us with live grenades yet. That would come later. Some threw the grenade like a baseball, others like a football and some with the swinging overhead motion of the arm as instructed. Most of us missed hitting our targets, but that was of no importance now.

Later we would all develop our own techniques and proficiency. Some would throw for distance, but most would hold the grenade ready to chuck into a cave opening just a few feet away. Some threw the grenade immediately after the pin was pulled, and others held it in their hand as the primer charge fizzed and smoked and counted, 'one', 'two,' and then threw. The explosion would occur in four or five seconds, the DI had said. Most of us did not trust that timing and got rid of it fast.

We saw some kids, without training or because of fear, throw the grenade without even pulling the pin during combat.

◆   ◆   ◆

Many Boots were not able to complete training because of physical and mental stress. They were either discharged or sent to other military units. One of the most stressful training exercise was the use of the gas mask. It gave the DIs another opportunity to weed out the ranks.

But before that we had our Sunday off. Sundays were reserved for reading, washing uniforms and cleaning equipment in general. We were young, we smoked, we ate candy and cake from home, and read and wrote letters. Those sweet Sundays were the most fleeting hours of our lives.

One can't appreciate water and food unless he has been deprived of them for a long period, and one cannot appreciate a Sunday unless he has been deprived of a week of freedom. Too quickly Sunday became Monday, the day of the gas mask drill.

Our gas masks were leftovers from the previous war's design It was made of canvas, had two glass eyepieces, a circular respirator, and straps for securing it around the back of the head tightly to keep out the gas. It was very rudimentary and questionably effective under serious gas conditions. We knew that during the previous war many were killed or wounded by mustard gas often in spite of using this equipment.

Our platoon was marched to the gas testing building which was a large, barn like structure made of corrugated metal. We were instructed in donning and removing the mask until we could do it with ease after a little practice. The important thing according the DI was to make sure the mask fit firming on your face against the cheeks to prevent gas from seeping in.

"Pull the straps behind your head real tight", he said.

It was hard to breathe with the mask tightly pressed against your face, and trying to breathe through the respirator. I had claustrophobia when my mask was on and my vision restricted. I could not imagine being able to function in combat conditions wearing that confining contraption that reduced breathing ability.

Others felt the same.

"When you get in the building we will release some tear gas and tell you to put on your masks. You will do as you were shown here today," the DI said.

"When the gas is cleared you will be instructed to remove your masks, but before you do you should test the air by opening one side of the mask away from your cheek to test the air condition. If it is clear you remove the mask."

"Got it?"

We all shook our heads affirmatively. But the DI wanted verbal acknowledgement.

"I can't **h-e-a-r** you," he said.

"**Yes sir**," we answered.

It was a simple series of instructions. They yell gas, you put on your mask. They stop the gas, you test to make sure it has stopped. If you don't smell gas, you remove your mask. Simple.

We entered the large metal building through two metal doors that were slammed shut behind us.

When we were inside, a voice over a loud speaker announced, "GAS."

The large building began to slowly fill with tear gas and we nervously fumbled with our mask straps and buckles to fit the contraptions over our heads for protection. Under the pressure of seeing the gas fill the room we took more time than necessary and some of us did not fit the masks properly and allowed the tear gas to enter the mask.

Men were choking and crying and coughing, but most seemed to be in good shape. I was a little uncomfortable having taken in some gas but was more worried about the gas filling the room, reducing visibility and creating a panic.

After several minutes that seemed like hours the loud speaker announced, "All clear, no more gas."

Some forgot the instruction to test the air by opening the mask slightly on one side first and were surprised that the gas was not completely clear when they removed the mask entirely. The remaining gas choked them and burned their eyes as they tried to don the mask again. Even we who waited for a while after testing as instructed, and then removing our masks, found the air still burned our eyes and choked our lungs.

Many of us were in some level of panic. One small kid we all called "Chicken" because of his size, was crying for his mother. I was embarrassed for him, but I could appreciate his fear. In various degrees we all shared it. Men were banging on the steel doors to be let out but they did not open. Whoever was in charge of the training for tear gas took his time opening the large door. Did they do this purposely? Of course. If they had let us out quickly what would we have learned? We all wanted desperately to be out of that building as quickly as possible. It was only a matter of time before we would all be banging at the door to get out.

When it was over we laughed embarrassingly about it just like we would laugh whenever we escaped another dangers. But of all the war games, the brief tear gas drill was the most stressful and humiliating because it stripped us of our self esteem, and induced a subtle fear.

Years later I read about the concentration camps and gas chambers in Europe where people who were gassed were found clustered in groups as they climbed on each other rushing for the exit door. I could compassionately appreciate their panic after my small experience during war games.

◆　　　◆　　　◆

The training continued with obstacle course runs through barbed wire, rope climbing over water hazards, all day marches with one canteen of water, swims with full back pack, and 30 mile marches.

DI punishments continued. Men were ordered to brush the barracks floors and toilets with a toothbrush, men told to sleep on a bed of rifles because they had dropped one, men told to fill their packs with sand and march for long hours for some infraction, or men holding buckets over their heads shouting, "I'm a shit head," were all common.

We washed our gear and scrubbed our boots and smeared the tough leather with grease to soften it. We polished our rifles and took them apart and oiled them day after day although they were never loaded, but soon they would be.

Now we were getting near the end of our training. There seemed to be a slightly more benevolent demeanor about the DIs. Their shouting was not as loud. There remained one part of our training before we were finished and that was qualifying with the M1 rifle as a marksman, sharpshooter or expert. The last days of the training would have us at the rifle range where for the first time we would be introduced to live ammunition and taught to shoot.

We learned to fire from the standard positions, standing, sitting and lying prone. We fired at targets at a distance so that we could not determine if we hit or missed. Someone in the target pits would have to signal with a flag where the shot had hit or missed, and a score would be tallied.

I made sharpshooter a few points below expert, but really don't know why. During this phase of the training rifle range instructors were in charge, not the DIs. These instructors taught with calmness and patience and it was a relief to be under their orders. Perhaps that is why we did well. I wondered if all the previous war games would not have been better played under the same conditions.

One day on the range I was told to report to the DI office and I was afraid I had done something wrong. I wanted no close contact with any DI if I could help it.

Knocking at the door I shouted, "Boot asks permission to see the Drill Instructor, Sir."

To humiliate you and keep you on edge, they never gave permission to enter until you repeated the request several times, or they pretended not to hear you so that you would have to shout for permission again. Finally permission would be granted to enter the room.

"Your mother is here to see you," the DI told me when I stood at attention before him.

I was speechless, surprised, embarrassed and angry.

The last time I had seen her was a dark morning near Christmas of 1938 when she came into my bedroom while my brother and I were sleeping to tell us she was leaving the family. My brother was ten, and I, two years older.

She had written to the Marine Corps requesting permission to see me, explaining her situation.

I don't know how much the DI knew, but he asked me how long had it been since I had seen my mother and why I had not written to her. He seemed satisfied with my answer,

My mother was thirty four at the time and attractive. We were allowed to be together for a few hours for lunch and I could see the Marines were having a good time looking at her attractive figure as we walked together. They probably wondered who the Boot was with the good looking woman.

I felt awkward with her and I could not wait for the visit to end. She enjoyed the attention she was getting from the men as usual, and I resented that too. She cried during most of the visit. She was so full of guilt, and I could understand why. The last time she had seen me I was twelve years old.

When she left, I returned to the rifle range where our training was completed. The DI did not reveal my mother's visit to the other men or I would have gotten a good ribbing for being a mommy's boy. To the contrary, it was because of her desertion that I was very self sufficient. But I never trusted anything again, including the Marine Corps. I was also very compassionate to those who suffered injustice.

◆   ◆   ◆

And so it was over. We were issued our green dress uniforms with emblem of globe, eagle and anchor, a symbol that we now belonged to the Corps. Once a Marine always a Marine and all that gung ho crap.

On the parade ground again this day the sun was still hot as ever and the government owned gnats were out too but we did not seem to notice it. The Drill Instructors were actually smiling and shaking everyone's hand and calling us by our last names, not, "shit heads". The ranking officer on the platform was saying nice things about us and how proud they all were.

He called us Marines.

I said, "bull shit!".

Then the band started to play that frigging hymn, and the scarlet and gold banner of the Corps with globe, anchor and eagle, flapped against the Stars and Stripes as the color bearers marched into view.

"From the halls of Montezuma, to the shores of Tripoli, we fight…" the music played.

I knew it was all show business, propaganda, bull shit, and part of war games. I knew that, but despite myself, I had tears in my eyes.

And when I looked along the line of young kids in green, they had tears in their eyes too.

◆   ◆   ◆

The small group of us who trained together and live and die in these pages came together by chance of the alphabet which put those with last names beginning with K and L in the same unit. We had all volunteered to join the Marines by free choice. This fact would be pointed out to us over and over during our enlistment years.

"You asked for it, no body forced you to join the Marines."

The few months of training had changed me. I could feel a self confidence that was not there before. Whether valid or not, I don't know. My painful shyness and sensitivity, however, still remained.

◆   ◆   ◆

Let's take the roll call of the boys who were with me.

Kruplowski, Dan Pvt. USMCR "Krup" "HERE!"

Hi, my name is Kruplowski. I'm the oldest of this group. I'm a year or so older than they are. I'm Polish, from Pennsylvania. My name is hard to remember unless you say it often. My buddies call me "Krup"

I have a girl friend in Quincy, Mass. where I worked in one of those shipyards as a welder's helper. I'm about six four, two hundred pounds, and I played football in high school. A little after the war started my brother got me a job in the Quincy shipyards. I lived in Quincy with him, his wife and kids. That's where I met Wanda. We plan to get married after the war.

My parents were immigrants and spoke little English and we followed the old customs until my brothers and sisters got older. Then we started to become more Americanized. But we still liked to eat kielbasa, pierogies and all the other Polish foods of our childhood. We have a large family of aunts and uncles who get together for birthday celebrations, holidays and funerals too. We belonged to the Greek Orthodox Church and have a lot of fun during church celebrations when all the women of the congregation got together to cook our favorite foods.

I was glad Wanda was Polish too because we had a lot in common and could speak about a lot of things that we experienced as kids. I love Wanda and wrote to her every day I could when we went overseas.

After working hard all week and making some overtime money for Saturday night fun, me and Wanda like to go out dancing and I put away a few beers and listen to the big band music on the juke boxes. Before going home we knew a place that we could park the car and neck for a while. Wanda and me loved each other and talked about our wedding plans and the family we would have. We never went all the way. Wanda would not allow that. We went far enough to make us both happy and feel that we had a good time. This way Wanda did not have to feel guilty about things. You know, family and church and all that stuff.

Whenever I was not with her I could still recall how she looked and smelled. I would go over in my mind how sweet her kisses were and how wonderful it was to hold her in my arms. She had that clear, white delicate Polish skin and blue eyes and blond hair that I loved to touch and kiss.

After a date I would take her home and kiss her good night. I did that the night before they told me to report to Boston to catch a train for Parris Island.

By the way, when you read this I will have been dead for over sixty years. I never got to grow old, have children or even get back to Wanda in Massachusetts.

You'll read about how it happened that night. So sudden, I didn't know what happened and no body else did either. So fast, I didn't have time to even pray or think of Wanda.

You know, I didn't have to join the Marines. I had a defense job and could be been deferred. I made good money too. Look at this pay stub I keep in my wallet. Close to one hundred dollars for the week counting twenty hours overtime. Not bad for a big Pollack eh?

My buddy Lance is the writer of our group and he will eventually tell you all about what happened to us. He had one of those Dago names but it was changed. We all called him Lance. He was always reading poetry from a paperback book he carried with him. Even in combat he read that book of English poetry and insisted at times to read it aloud. He was a nice kid, honest, loyal friend, figured out the angles quickly, took all the short cuts. I think he was more of a poet than a fighting Marine. He was a very good kid and cried like hell the day I got it.

Lance, Joseph Pvt. USMCR, "Lance the Poet", "Here!"

You can call me Lance, or Poet, if you like. Lance was my Americanized name.

My dog tags are stamped C for Catholic, I'm not really. My name used to be Italian and the government of the United States says American. I'm neither really, at heart. I feel my nationality is not defined by geographical location but the world does. I'm ahead of my time in ways for a dumb kid, and very cautious of the world too.

Most of us weren't going anywhere in this world in 1939 the year I graduated elementary school. I was in a one parent home and that parent was making fifteen dollars a week, when he worked in the Works Progress Administration, WPA, as a laborer digging ditches in various parts of New Jersey.

I was ashamed of him and his occupation and our poverty until I read more and understood where we fit into this thing, this country, this system we call America.

I hated high school. I was not bright, or big enough to play varsity sports. I had pimples that made shy away from the other kids, especially the girls. I had poor clothes to wear to class and often had to steal a shirt from a neighbor's clothesline to attend school.

After school was a different thing. I loved to play all sports just for the fun of it. Winning or losing were not as important to me as just playing. I took great joy in using my young body, running, jumping, throwing balls, hitting balls, kicking balls. The pure, animal joy of movement was fun. I loved reading books, and wanted to read all the books in the world. But I did not want to memorize parts of them to repeat in a test. I wrote poetry that would bring tears to my eyes as I read them, but they were mostly bad poems which I destroyed over the years. I read Thoreau at sixteen. Learned about civil disobedience. Questioned and distrusted authority. Sought a simple life.

I always felt that something would happen in my life that would rescue me from boredom and deliver me into a world of excitement. I just kept waiting and waiting for something big to happen. The Marines gave me that chance.

LaForse, Louis J. Pvt. USMCR—'LaFoo' "Here!"

Louie never speaks much, never did, so I'll just have to tell you about him as I remembered his stories and his time with us.

We call him LaFoo playfully most of the time. He likes playing the simple, fun loving, devil may care Frenchman He found his place in the world when he joined the Marines at seventeen. He enjoyed Parris Island and the tough training. After Boot training he enjoyed liberties and getting drunk and fighting with sailors and coming back to the base bleeding and dirty. He wore his uniform with a cocky pride, all five feet six and a half inches of him all hard and mean.

To me he was the Wolf Larson character Jack London created, tough, very tough. He loved to break things. Returning from liberty drunk and mad he'd punch walls and doors until his hands bled. He loved to brawl in the bar rooms and then display his bruised face as proudly as his bruised knuckles.

He walked and stood with a firmness as though he was one with the earth, immoveable. Silent, cocky, strong, he drank anything that had alcohol in it and then would sing ribald, French Canadian songs roaring out the curse words with laughter. He was a devout Catholic.

During The Depression up in the mountains of northern New Hampshire many families relied on the hunting skills of the family men to bring home meat for the table. That meat and the small patches of gardens that grew vegetables were the source of food that meant a better life. Hunting was more a necessity than sport.

LaFoo was what he liked to call with pride, 'a French Canuck', a mixture of American Indian, French and American bloods that produced a hearty people at times, and at times otherwise. It was the blood of America often mingled through rape, lust, hunger, and occasionally, love.

LaFoo had been trained by his father, uncles and other members of the extended family to hunt in the rugged mountains. He hunted before he was ten, so at the time he enlisted in the Marines, he had a good background for stalking and shooting in the woods.

"You never leave a wounded animal to die alone in the woods if you know that you hit him with a shot," he would explain when discussing his favorite topic. You track him until you find him even if it takes days. Then you kill it. Don't make it suffer."

After a kill he had to butcher the animal and pack it so that he could carry it back to his mother who was expecting him to return with food. There was always the fear of returning home without a kill. Killing animals was very important to him.

During one hunt he tracked a wounded deer for most of a day before it was found and killed. LaFoo, his body half frozen, and his stomach rumbling hours after digesting the biscuit and bacon he had for breakfast, slit open the belly of the big buck and scraped the steaming guts into the snow. He cut out the liver and other parts that were choice and ate some of the beast raw.

On the rifle range he shot 'expert'.

◆ ◆ ◆

Long, James D. Private USMCR 'JD' "Here!"

I'm about five feet nine, and a good dresser. I like looking good in my uniform just as I liked looking good in civilian cloths. My uniforms always fit like they were tailored. My hair is never out of place. Neatly trimmed and dark. black, "Black Irish" that's what I am.

I like my uniform to fit me just right. If I have time I pay a tailor to adjust them for me. I keep my uniforms neat, and pleat my shirts so they fall squarely into my pants without bulging. I don't like wrinkles, and I spit shine my shoes until I can see my face in them. It takes a lot of time, but I do it. You notice how my hat fits me just square on my head and clean cut. There are no bulges and creases and the emblems are polished just enough to highlight the globe and eagle. I do that with a little polishing cloth. It's what we call the salty look.

When they issue these uniforms to us they are just hanging on our bones. You have to have them fitted and you have to press them right if you want to look good. The girls notice it right away.

I'm from Philly and I know a little about the tough world. The world is mainly the rich against the poor. My grandfather told me about the British rule of Ireland and how they starved the people out. Now they want Ireland to join in and fight this war for them.

I know that the first wave of Irish immigrants fought in the Civil War and were often used as substitutes for those who had money. What the hell, we survived.

I go to Mass every Sunday and on the holy days of obligation too. I have a few girl friends who are good Catholic girls and Irish. My mother likes that and my sisters kid me about them. I love my family very much and can't wait to get back to them, get married and have a family. I write to several girl friends when I get a chance, but I have a particular favorite, Deirdre.

Deirdre studied with the nuns in parochial school and was very religious. Sometimes I think too religious. She confessed everything we did on our dates to Father Dunn and was glad to do penance for forgiveness. We argued over that. I never thought we did anything that required forgiveness. That's why I think she is special to me.

My father drives a sanitation truck for the city. He has the brains to do much more but can't get a break. It's who you know these days and we don't know too many people who have pull in city hall. I have a bunch of pals around my neighborhood and they are from all backgrounds. Pollacks, Dagos, even a few blacks and we get along.

◆   ◆   ◆

A photograph taken of us together on liberty at the Grand Hotel in San Diego before going overseas, shows four kids in Marine uniforms trying to act grown up.

The hotel photographer worked fast knowing that we would all buy a copy to send home. We are sitting around a table cluttered with beer bottles, glasses and ash trays. Everyone has his field scarf hanging loose and collar open except JD. Big Krup is in the center smiling and raising a glass of beer in a toast, to his left LaFoo is caught with a bottle to his lips, to Krup's right, JD, neat and dapper, holds a whisky glass. He is feeling no pain. And there all by himself and almost out of the photo, the poet, smiling shyly wishing the cameraman leaves him out. We all have a cigarette smoking in our hand, lips, or ash tray, just as we learned from the movies.

The chubby waitress stands behind us smiling in her yellow and brown 1944 uniform with the tiny white apron, holding an empty tray of bottles and glasses. She is old, maybe twenty nine, or even thirty. She is about to leave the scene and escape the photographer's view but is caught by the lens. Her captured image joins us, and will greet us whenever we look at that photo, and remind us how young and innocent we were.

2

Guard Duty, Boston

You will walk your post in a military manner. You will not sleep or leave your post. You will salute the officer of the guard. You will…General Orders for Guard Duty USMC.

I had applied for Sea Duty when they passed out the duty preference forms. I was just a naïve and uneducated kid who would never be chosen for such and elite assignment. Sea Duty Marines were tall and clean cut and educated. They did not look like ghetto kids and they spoke well. They were supposed to look good standing on guard at the Tomb of the Unknown Soldier, on board big naval ships, and the U.S. Embassies throughout the world.

It took me a while to realize I was just a cannon fodder Marine. A rifleman, the bottom of the barrel, the guys they send to face the enemy in person. Sea Duty was for special people.

After Boot Camp we got orders to return home to show off our uniforms and have our families see us alive once more before we reported for guard duty assignments in Boston. It was not Sea Duty, but it was a little better than going to advance training and overseas. The government was allowing us to live our young lives a little longer before putting us at risk. It was a good feeling for young kids in 1944 to wear a uniform. Of course the older men and women knew how dangerous uniforms could be having lived through the previous war but they kept those thoughts to themselves. We would not have understood anyway.

We had a fist full of green backs in our pockets that we never had before. Perhaps as much as fifty dollars or a little more. We could go to the local hangouts with confidence strutting in our uniforms before our friends, especially the girls.

Uncle Sam had supplied us with money, and in three months the various services had transformed us from sad looking and vulnerable kids into eager young men wanting to serve. We were perhaps a little over confident, and little too proud of uniforms.

Ten days leave went fast with a series of family parties and amateurish encounters with girl friends. The time came and went with the same fleeting sigh of time that always has been. Many of us who had last names starting with K and L, were sent to do guard duty at Boston Navy Yard just as those letters had grouped us together in Parris Island.

Most of us had never traveled more than a few miles from our home towns. I had been to New York to see the Worlds Fair of 1939 with my elementary school class. Now we were on our own and on our way to Boston. We were not in a group and had no Drill Instructor to shout at us at every turn. We were making a train trip from our homes to Boston in war time, and it was exciting.

The six hour train ride from New York to Boston's South Street Station was the same as many trips along that route during the war. The train was blacked out and only a dim light shown inside the compartments that were filled with military men and women from the various services. Young kids, some not shaving regularly, and some with adolescent acne just beginning to clear from high school days, made up most of the crowd packed into the coach cars. Some arranged their seats so that they could face each other and have a game of poker, others cleared a small area where they could roll dice, most just sat and talked, smoked and drank beer and soda.

A lucky Marine or sailor would be hunched in one of the rear seats where it was darkest or in the platform between trains busy trying to make love to a young woman he had just met as the train lurched side to side. When this was happening no one bothered the couple and gave them a lot of space if they could. Sometimes if necessary, a jacket or coat would be thrown over the lovers and they were as good as in a private room.

This was the romantic, brief encounter, of the enlisted man during the long train rides across America. No lingering kisses on the platform and sad waves goodbye. Time was short and if two people sought and found momentary solace and love in a blacked out train, no one was gong to object or judge. The newly met lovers would only be entangled in a series of long embraces during the trip and then they left each other forever.

The tight compartments always smelled of spilled beer, urine from the overflowing toilets, cigarette smoke and perspiration. Almost everybody smoked and drank at least a beer. No one had deodorants to protect his fellow passengers, but there was plenty of shaving lotion and perfume.

Unlike the train ride to Parris Island just three short months before, we were now traveling as independent military men. After Boot Camp we were expected to know what to do and carry out orders as assigned, but we were not sophisticated by any imagination. We had a great deal yet to learn about the world.

Krup, LaFoo, JD, and I, were all assigned to do guard duty at Boston Navy Yard.

Alphabetically, was the easiest way to transfer men after you had screen them according to their talents. We were all about the same age and about the same level of education and skills. We were just average kids with strong bodies.

South Street Station was cluttered, dark, crowded and full of activity including the exciting announcements of train arrivals and departures. The trains to Rhode Island, Maine, New Hampshire, Canada, New York were all announced over the PA system. I felt part of a wonderful, exciting world where so much was going on.

In just a few months we had been to Washington, South Carolina, New York, Philadelphia, and now Boston. We were seeing the world. Military personnel were reporting to various parts of the country for duty, and civilians were traveling for the same mundane reasons they did in peace time, deaths in the family, relocation to jobs, visits to families. Each of us was concerned with our own lives as we passed each other briefly on the station platforms.

When we reported for our guard duty assignment we began to mix with Marines from other units. Many veteran Marines who had just returned from the fighting at Guadalcanal were among us and we looked upon these veterans with awe. They were several years older than we and we had remembered seeing the Guadalcanal movies that depicted their experiences and that induced many of us to enlist. These were the real men who were there, not movie actors, and we were excited to be in their company.

Marines were always aware of their seniority status defined as so many months or years since Boot Camp. It was a measure we took of each other, as kids do in high school and college sorting freshmen from sophomores and juniors from seniors. This status comparison would continue until the first combat experience which would make us all equal.

We felt ludicrously sophisticated and worldly in our new, ill fitting uniforms that did not fit us properly, but the people welcomed us because they too had sons, brothers and husbands in the service. Everyone had someone serving somewhere in the country or the world. We were 'the boys in service.'

The Guadalcanal veterans' uniforms, however, fit them with more style since they had been in the Corps longer and had tailors to adjust the fit properly. Their tailored uniforms were cut perfectly and did not bulge and sag like ours. They also they had a row of multi-colored ribbons on their jackets identifying Pacific battles, and medal awards, and this added a splash of heroic color.

We all clogged the streets and roadways around Boston holding our thumbs in the air hitch hiking from place to place on liberty. Rides were easy to get. The country was more like one big family in this respect. Talk came easy and the smiles too. We were all involved and that made a difference. The old man who gives you a lift had a son in Europe, he tells you. Another tells you about his boy in the Pacific, or training in Florida or Texas. We were facing a common crisis and it bound us together.

Part of our guard duty assignments included posts in nearby Squantum Naval Air Station where we were assigned to barracks. This was a large, a very active military airfield and consisted mainly of barracks and hangers and all the other infrastructure necessary to accommodate military aircraft activity. It was only a few miles from Boston Navy Yard which had the more impressive buildings where the top brass had offices.

We went to Boston where we spent our money like kids at the carnival, walking aimlessly about the streets of Scully Square looking for girls and bargain trinkets to send home. At times we had forty or even fifty dollars in our pockets itching to be spent after pay call. The wonders of Boston, especially Scully Square, with its joints, clubs, and shows was the main attraction for most.

We filled the streets and walked aimlessly and pathetically until late at night and early morning. Army, Navy, Marines, Seabees, and Air Force kids just hanging out and being enticed by hawkers. Military Police roamed in and out of the crowd doing their duty, intimidating would be troublemakers.

Lilli St.Cyr, the burlesque queen, was appearing for a long run and her larger than life photo beckoned us to buy tickets to see her act. She was one of the top burlesque queens at the time, and it cost a buck or two to see her in action with her fans and doves. We roared appreciatively when she allowed a peek of her breasts, but the shows were tame.

Many called Scully Square a zoo as the military personnel roamed through the streets, some half drunk on a couple of beers. Most of the citizens of Boston were in their beds resting for the coming workday. Only a few girls were out at that hour and they were either professionals or young kids just too stupid and lonely to go home.

When the money ran out or we tired of Scully Square we would go to the Canteen which was located at Boston Common. At the Canteen the woman and young girls from the area volunteered to talk and dance with servicemen who were feeling lonely and needed a little company. Coffee and doughnuts where always available and a place to sit and read magazines too. Mostly we went there to look at the young women. The times were lonely and desperate, and we sought human contact to pass the hours.

As always, the swan boats carrying passengers glided in the Boston Common lake adding a little joy to those sad and serious days. If you were lucky you had a girl to share the ride with you.

I met Phyllis at one of the Canteen dances. She taught me to drink Singapore Slings, ride in a taxi and kiss with touching tongues. Phyllis was two years older than I and was a secretary who had boy friends before. She was sophisticated. I followed her instructions. We were friends for a few weeks and she introduced me to her family who was vacationing near Plymouth that summer of 1944.

It was a war summer vacation for the family and I felt a certain sadness about the older people. They looked at me with a forced pleasantness, knowing that it was all so temporary and they would probably not see me again after that day. Everything was temporary, transient, sad and precarious. Any moment orders could arrive that would send you away. They had sons and fathers and brothers in the same situation so they were extra kind.

We who were young were excited about everything that was happening in those days that came and disappeared like a series of magical tricks. We did not dwell on the danger that was awaiting us on the other side of the world, and that we were reminded about in each evening radio news. We focused on the fun we found in each other at the moment and did not look too deeply into the days to come.

During our few weeks of friendship we fell in 'love', and fought, and broke up, and made up, and fought again. I was sorry after one break up especially since just a few days earlier we had made a love song a part of our 'endless' friendship. The song was, *Together*.

'*They walked in the rain together, laughed in the rain together…we will always be together.*'

It was a forties hit that is played at times today when radio programs recall that time. When they do, it brings back memories so far in the past that I question their validity. How could anyone have been so young and innocent? Yet the intensity of youth is very genuine as it is lived, and only discounted when appraised from the wisdom of an older age.

Our five week 'love affair' which consisted of perhaps seven dates, was over. We had made no commitments. We were all making our own grade B Hollywood movies and moving on.

I barely made it to the front gate to check in at Squantum Naval Air Station that night after liberty. I had hitchhiked from Newtonville, a suburb of Boston, to the barracks and rushed through the gates showing my pass just in time. I got to my bunk and nearly passed out from fatigue and two Singapore Slings. I was up again within a few short hours to stand guard duty.

"Fall in," the sergeant shouted in that cold morning of October 1944 and marched us to the flag raising ceremony which was conducted every day at dawn wherever there are American military men throughout the world. During the ceremony a cold, Canadian wind was blowing around the small column of men standing at attention. The bugle blew, "To The Colors", and the flag was quickly raised to the top of the mast.

Most of us in line had been on liberty the night before and were not too alert in spite of drinking a hot cup of Marine coffee. The sun was barely making it over the horizon and the wind was whipping the red, white and blue with a snapping sound you could hear a distance away.

"Look at Old Glory flying like a son of bitch," someone whispered irreverently, resenting being up so early to watch a flag raising. We understood his annoyance, and chuckled. We had never heard Old Glory described in those words, and only a person who promised to die defending it could get away with it.

Cold and tired, we still appreciated seeing the flag in the air with its two corners whipping the wind. I still can become emotional watching the red, white and blue banner against the cold sky in spite of trying at times to be aloof of these nationalistic symbols. I hated myself for that at times, but it was indoctrinated in me as child, I guess.

I visualized flag raisings around the world as the dawn inched its way around our spinning earth. Every day at dawn the flag would be raised by Americans all over the world from jungle to arctic, on land and sea. The bugles would sound the Call To Colors and the flag would sit at the top of the mast. Ships in the Atlantic had already gone through the observance and we were doing it now at Squantum.

Three hours later, California's dawn would demand another Call to Colors, and the bugle would sound, and the Stars and Stripes would be run up flagpoles by the thousands at every base, on every ship, land and sea.. This would continue across the Pacific and around again, repeating the ritual tomorrow, here, where we stood.

After raising the colors we had one of those good, greasy Marine breakfasts and went to the barracks duty roster to see where we would stand guard duty for the day. I was overtired and hung over, and in poor condition to stand guard.

My post was located at an ammunition dump way out across the airfield near the marshes where the ammunition was underground and covered by mounds of earth works. It was a lonely, desolate and cold post.

My duty for four hours was to walk among the mounds of the ammunition fields and look alert in case any intruder wanted to blow up the ammunition, I guess. No one told men exactly what to do. It was a desolate place remote from the main base by several miles, and soon I got tired and bored with the guard duty. The only diversion was the landing of sea gulls that constantly circled over head, and the distant and take offs and landings of Navy airplanes.

I talked to the gulls just to hear the sound of my own voice. The loneliness and monotony of being in that enormous airfield was eerie. I felt I was lost in a strange world of grassy dunes and gulls.

I was scheduled to walk this post for four hours with a sub-machine gun slung over my shoulder. It was a Rising sub-machine gun that I had never fired. It was a light piece with a folding stock that was made of a tough steel band that could be folded forward so the gun could be fired from the hip or folded back so that it could be rested into the shoulder and fired that way.

It was loaded with a clip of ammunition that held .45 caliber bullets. It had poor accuracy at a long distance but had powerful stopping power at close range, I was told. Semi automatic, it could be fired one shot at a time, or in bursts, spraying an area with fat, forty five caliber bullets. It could do a lot of damage but the need to shoot at anyone in this guard post was pretty remote.

One fat sea gull made a tempting target walking slowing along one of the ammunition mounds and I was bored enough to want to shoot it. I was not more than thirty feet from the bird when I lifted the gun to my shoulder and aimed. Surprisingly the sound of the shot did not seem loud. I missed, and the bird took off slowly, frightened by the bullet that hit several inches from where it stood. I noticed the kick of the piece was not too hard and I felt good that I had checked it out. Now I knew how it felt. If anyone had heard and investigated I would say it was an accident.

I had been on duty for about two hours and was beginning to feel really weary and cold. I had slept little the night before, and the cold, October day in New England was sucking away my strength. My hands and feet were cold and so was my face as I walked up and down the long rows of ammo mounds only partially protected from the wind.

As I turned around to make another pass along the route I had taken I noticed that a small guard shack was located along the road and that smoke was coming out of the small, tin chimney. It looked inviting and I investigated. At the door I saw that the small hut had a oil stove, table, chairs and a small cot.

It looked so cozy and warm. What the hell. Who would know? Who would care if I sat down for a few minutes and warmed myself by that fire. I knew that I could not trust myself to lie down on the cot it would be too comfortable for me to leave.

I was just going to sit for a minute to get warm, and then go back out into the cold. Just one minute, or even less, I promised myself, and then I would come out of that warm hut. I was just going to sit on the edge of the cot. I felt the warmth of the stove ease into my body, and my muscles relaxed as though I were in a warm bath. The warmth drained all the weariness and cold from me like an hypnotic spell.

One of general orders for walking guard duty, even I knew, was to walk your post in a military manner. You do not sit your post, you walk it. Military manner does not mean slouching and shooting at birds. It means standing straight and dignified as you walk.

In spite of the orders, I could not help myself and within seconds I was sound asleep. This was no ordinary sleep but a sound, drugged state of unconsciousness.

It seemed like a few seconds had passed since I had promised myself not to remain long. And it seemed like an eternity of warmth and happy coma that was interrupted by some one shouting in my face.

"Get up, asshole, What the hell are you doing sleeping on guard duty?"

It was the sergeant of the guard who had made his rounds and found me in the hut. Of course the sergeant or the corporal who accompanied him had taken my gun from my hands as I slept, proving I had lost control of my weapon. A terrible offense. I did not even feel the gun removed from my hands. If an enemy had taken it I would be dead.

"They're going to hang your ass for this one, shit head, sure as hell, they are going to hang your ass high."

The sergeant and the corporal were both veterans of the Guadalcanal campaign and this compounded my shame. I was so embarrassed that I began to blush when I realized that I had been caught sleeping by veterans of Guadalcanal. My shame prevented me from uttering a word of explanation which would have been worthless anyway.

On Guadalcanal, as anywhere, sleeping on post is a very seriously offense that jeopardized lives. These men had experienced many days of fighting on that island and they knew the seriousness of my error. They were not considering that I was alone in a remote ammo dump, bored and cold. They did not care that I was still almost a Boot. Sleeping on post is the same offense, combat or stateside, veteran or Boot.

"Put this man under arrest," the sergeant told the corporal who grasped me roughly by my sleeve and lifted me to my feet.

"You're under arrest Marine, follow me."

They walked me to the Jeep that was idling softly in the cold, sending a mist of exhaust into the brittle Massachusetts air. We drove back to headquarters where they placed me in a detention room waiting for formal charges and court martial proceedings. Just twenty four hours ago I was enjoying my last date with Phyllis.

I remembered what the Drill Instructor said about the rifle in Boot Camp, how important it was and that you guarded it with your life. Well I forgot that rule and it was going to cost me. They could shoot you if you broke that general order, especially if you were in a war zone. I was so young and innocent that I would have walked in front of a firing squad then and there if they ordered me.

They marched me to the brig and prepared me for a Court Martial. That was all I had to know. It was like a bad dream and I expected to wake up from it with the happiness of knowing it was only a dream. I did not wake up and it was not a dream.

There was no pleading of my case. No one asked me if I had an excuse. Was I sick? Did I know about the shack being off limits? Hell. I was caught sleeping by two Guadalcanal veterans. What more did you need?

The next day they drove me to the main square of the Boston Navy Yard where they had gathered a detachment of Marines and sailors to witness my shame and disgrace. I was dressed in the Marine green dress uniform and marched to the center of the square and brought to a halt. I wore a jacket and no coat. The October sun shown brightly but the air still had that New England briskness to it.

Nearby Old Ironsides, The Constitution, lay in her berth, a proud part of the country's history.

In fact, I knew the poem that Oliver Wendell Holmes wrote to save Old Ironsides from destruction.

"Aye tear her tattered ensign down, long has it waved on high…for many an eye has danced to see that banner in the sky."

Just outside the Navy Yard, was Bunker Hill which was crowned with the obe-lisk monument that carried the words we learned in grammar school, "Don't fire until you see the whites of their eyes."

The Boston area was a museum of American history. The Old North Church where they were to raise the lanterns, one if by land, two if by sea, Paul Revere riding at midnight to warn the countryside, the Tea Party, and not far away, the Concord Bridge, where Emerson said, "…was fired the shot heard around the world."

I had sullied these proud moments of our history.

Ordered to stand at attention in front of all these men brought shame to my heart. They played the Marine Hymn, this time I had no tears. Then read the charges. "Deserting his post, sleeping on duty."

I caught fragments of words that my brain did not want to remember. My dis-tress was especially painful because I was an introverted kid and did not like to be put on display. Authority had me in its control and could destroy me if it willed, and I wished it would. I could not wait until they marched me off somewhere, anywhere.

All the old movies of the French Foreign Legion court martial scenes rushed to my mind. The court-martialed men were usually officers dressed in fancy uni-forms with all sorts of epaulets, stripes and ornaments that had to be removed. These were all torn away from the man until he remained in a stripped uniform, and then they broke his saber over their knee.

I was a Private. The only ornament on my uniform was the globe, anchor and eagle. One emblem on my cap, and two on my jacket. I had earned those emblems only a few weeks ago. No stripes to rip off, no saber to break, even in my own court martial I was a failure. A ludicrous child caught in the serious, bureaucratic mechanics of the military. I heard Thoreau whisper in my ear, "It's a game they play."

Ah dear Henry, this is some game.

Before my sentencing was read, an officer approached me formally and took the Marine emblems from my cap, and my jacket. I was in a green uniform with-out emblems and could have been just a sanitation man or any kind of worker required to wear a uniform of that material. Without the globe, eagle and anchor, the uniform meant nothing. They knew that, of course, and disgraced me. I stood there feeling naked and degraded.

Someone said, "eight days bread and water", and another said, "eight days piss and punk." They were the same thing. One was English and the other Marine and Navy talk.

Eight days bread and water? Was that the sentence?

"Eight days piss and punk," some Marines whispered.

I could not believe that it was happening, but it was, and then, to my relief, they marched me off at double time towards the brig. I knew the man who was marching behind me had been ordered to shoot me if I tried to escape or serve my sentence himself. I had been in his position before and knew the rules. I couldn't wait to get to the brig and out of public view, and had no intention of escaping anywhere.

I felt a great relief as I was marched from the onlookers, military and civilian, and the embarrassing pity in their eyes. I had served my purpose. The Marine Corps had made a example of me and disgraced me in front of my peers as I deserved. I could not plead that I was just a kid anymore. The authority of the Marine Corps over me was supreme and it would take a lot of guts and brains to survive that power.

At the brig I was issued a prisoner uniform with a big **P** painted on the back of the jacket. I was not issued a coat because I was not going outdoors. Eight days of piss and punk meant that you stayed in a cell and did not move from it. You did not talk to anyone and you did not need much to stay alive just a little bread and water three times a day.

I learned in the brig that there is something that brings men together following Marine training. We were from different sections of the country with varying ethnic and religious backgrounds who had experienced an intense training together. That shared experience created a bond of understanding and mutual respect.

My fellow prisoners who were permitted regular meals at the mess hall would return after chow, and as they passed my cell they would silently slip in pieces of chicken, an orange, and any other bit of food they could manage to conceal. They did this automatically without a plan, without my asking, without comment or indication of seeking thanks. They just did it and walked on to their own cells.

I would never ask anyone to steal food for me. I was too shy and proud for that and perfectly able to live on bread and water for eight days. There had been days in my eighteen years when I had little more than that.

Every day there was another bit of food surreptitiously handed to me as they passed my cell. I was glad to be on bread and water because I did not have to be marched to the mess hall under guard three times a day and gawked at with pity. Loss of pride was more painful than loss of some food.

I was full of moral codes instilled by cowboy movies. I should not jeopardize my benefactors. When I ate the orange they gave me, I ate it skin, pits and all, leaving nothing as evidence. Apples I ate whole, stems, pits, everything. I even chewed and swallowed the tiny chicken bones. The larger bones I slipped through the circular holes that were cut into the steel ceiling of the cell for ventilation.

From then on, whenever I had one of those thick skinned oranges from Californian, I would recalled those eight brig days. I would smile as I bit into the orange. Then as a ritual of remembrance, I would eat the whole damn thing, skin, pits and all.

Because of the kindness of my fellow prisoners I felt my pride returning. I felt that these guys also had made mistakes, and were overlooking mine, and accepting me as a friend. They understood an error could be made by any one. They did not punish me for it because I was paying my penalty. Perhaps it was also their way of rebelling against authority in general.

We were all just kids with a few men mixed in to give us some stability. Whatever little we thought we knew about life at eighteen years we had mostly learned from the movies.

One of the Guadalcanal Marines who arrested me came to my cell while he was on duty one day and asked how I was doing. I was proud, happy and embarrassed to see him. On his sleeve was the diamond patch with the big number one on it and the word Guadalcanal. That patch alone spoke a thousand words in those years. I felt humiliated.

"How are you doing, buddy," he asked?

He was only two or three years older than I.

Sheepishly I said, "okay."

He smiled and winked. We never saw each other again.

Several days later after my brig time was over. I was sitting around my bunk with Krup, LaFoo and Long telling about my experiences which had made me some sort of minor hero among my buddies. It made me salty, a Marine who had brig time. Of course they called me 'jail bird' and other names mostly deserved, but regarded me as a friend. The duty non com interrupted our bull session and told us a Navy fighter plane had crashed during a rain storm somewhere in Worcester which was about fifty miles away.

The duty non com told me that I and a Marine we called, "Chief", with respect, were chosen by the top sergeant to guard the crash site. It was a duty assignment you gave to someone you disliked. I knew I fit the qualifications but did not understand why Chief was included. Chief was an Indian kid from Oklahoma.

Chief spoke only if necessary and smiled grudgingly. He stood about six feet, four inches tall and was powerfully built, bronzed, and graceful in movement. He had jet black hair, and strong, white teeth, and a pock marked face.

We had shared liberty once when Phyllis asked me to bring a date for a girl friend. Her girl friend was a little surprised when she first met Chief but became accustomed to his lack of conversation. After a few beers Chief would relax and everything went well.

One night when we were returning late to the base, the main gate had been closed. Technically, we were away without leave, AWOL. We went to a dark area where there was no guard, but had an eight foot chain linked fence with three strands of barbed wire on the top in a slanted position toward the interior. We had to quickly climb the fence and make our way to the barracks before we were reported missing.

I weighed about a hundred and thirty five pounds and Chief had at least fifty pounds of muscle more than that. He used it to boost me up to the top and over the fence with one heave. I rolled over the wires unharmed, relying on my heavy overcoat to cushion the barbed wire. Then he scampered up and over the fence alone. I was impressed and amazed by his strength and agility, and told him so. He said nothing. We made it to the barracks in time, and then I noticed where the barbed wire had cut deeply into his arms and he was bleeding. He said nothing.

I was proud to be his friend especially because he was an Indian and had all that mystique about him that I had learned from the radio and movies. For me, Tonto and the Lone Ranger, Indian Scouts, and all the Indian heroes were rolled together into Chief.

Now we were sharing another adventure, riding in the back of a canvas covered truck to protect us from the cold rain as we headed for a crashed plane somewhere in the night. Civilian cars were in the streets with blacked out headlights going to destinations far more ordinary than ours. It took the driver a long time to find the crash site in a deeply wooded area away from the city.

The plane had crashed in a desolate place that was accessible only over dirt roads and wooded ground. As the driver switched gears back and forth to manage the terrain, the truck growled and protested its way toward the activity ahead of us. We could see large search lights illuminating the area into a surreal atmosphere of bright lights, eerie, exaggerated shadows of men in slickers, exhaust fumes and heavy rain.

Rescue crews played their lights into the tall trees where the aircraft had come through and where it was suspended on the top branches of smaller trees. The plane was about forty feet off the ground. The lights glared on the cockpit where rescue workers were trying to remove the pilot. They had a crane in position so that they could place a harness around the pilot to lift him from the cockpit. The canopy had been sheered off. As they lifted him out, one of his legs dangled and was about to come off at the knee. It hung by a piece of the man's skin and ligaments. His face was torn and bleeding. He was limp, hanging like a soft, stuffed, uniformed puppet in the grotesque glare.

The pilot's flight helmet and goggles had been torn from his head. They were hanging from one of the upper tree branches, glistening and dangling playfully out of reach like a child's toys. Various military and civilian personnel were milling about giving orders and clearing the site so that an ambulance could enter and take the pilot away. The tall trees hovered over us, the wind tossed their branches and sent cascades of rain down through the probing shafts of the searchlights.

Some civilian unit had prepared coffee and the smell of it permeated the woods mixing with the odor of gasoline fumes which drifted close to the ground. In an hour the activity ended. An ambulance carrying the pilot led a procession of vehicles that followed in a slow, grinding cortège, and then the area was cordoned off.

The gasoline fumes overwhelmed the coffee aroma, and the darkness returned to the night when the lights were gone. The searchlight trucks left last, leaving Chief and me alone in the rain. We were ordered not to allow anyone into the site for anything other than official business, and because of the gasoline fumes, not to smoke.

We sat with our backs against a large tree where the gas fumes were light, lit cigarettes with a Zippo, disregarding orders again, and felt the rain seep through our ponchos. Occasionally we sipped sparingly from our canteen of lukewarm coffee trying to make it last the night.

We did not speak to each other more than a few curse words about the rain and the cold. The words were mostly mine. In my mind was stamped the image of the mangled pilot, the first dead man of our war. I would recalled that image periodically as long as I lived.

In the light of a new day the tops of giant trees that had disappeared in the blackness returned. We looked up at the wrecked plane still suspended above us in the trees and saw some of the pilot's blood stained on the silver fuselage near the white, American star painted on it. On the ground we found a watch with broken crystal, the arms motionless, having recorded the end of the young pilot's life. We saw bits of his flesh and viscera, and splashes of blood that had belonged to him, and he was gone.

We had guard duty for over twelve hours and wondered if they had forgotten us. I suspected the sergeant of taking his revenge. We were in a very remote area and could not hear any sound of civilization, no distant motors humming, dogs barking, or cocks crowing to welcome the morning. We had no phone or radio. There was nothing to do but wait for orders and keep guarding the crashed fighter plane hanging above us in the trees.

Finally our relief guard came, and military crews started removing the aircraft from the trees, and inspecting the site for their reports. I wondered where the pilot had been taken and who was suffering because of his death.

◆　　　◆　　　◆

Several days later a group of us were sitting around the squad room shooting the bull, complaining, smoking, shining shoes and cleaning rifles.

Krup and Long were talking about their liberty adventures as JD was pressing one of his immaculate, and militarily perfect shirts making sure the creases were just right. I was sitting on the lower bunk cleaning my Rising sub machine gun, the one I had shot at the gull with, and Chief was across the squad room sitting on the lower bunk of his bed. He was just sitting there quiet and peaceful. He always had this solemn look that revealed nothing.

"I heard that we will be shipping out in a few days," Krup was saying, "you should have seen Wanda last night when I told her. She cried all night.".

I was oiling my weapon and cleaning the barrel with a rod, and wiping the .45 caliber bullets as I placed them in the clip feeling their sensual, stubby fatness in my fingers. When I finished cleaning, I put the clip in place and in doing so had placed one round in the firing chamber. The weapon was ready to kill someone if the safety was off, and it was.

Like a fool I began aiming the weapon around the squad room but not at any person. I was just swinging the barrel around the room looking down through the sights not realizing that the weapon was loaded and the safety was off. The rifle fired.

I don't remember pulling the trigger, but it fired, and made a loud report that startled everyone.

Across the room still sitting on his cot Chief grasped his left chest and looked up in surprise. He said nothing, he then stared at something in his right hand. I thought that I had shot him and that at any moment he was going to fall over dead. I was paralyzed with fear.

In his hand Chief held the fragments of the bullet. He was not hurt.

The company commander and his deputy came running in from their office which was just outside the main barrack and were asking about the shot. No one spoke. No one was sure what had happened.

The bullet had hit a steel bar on the bunk near where the Chief was sitting and pieces ricochet off and hit the Chief's chest. He reached for his chest and caught the fragments, clutching them in his hand. The fragments did not even penetrate his jacket. Just six inches to the right I would have blown his head off.

For some reason I don't know, the officers did not pursue the incident. Perhaps there was nothing you could do about a accidental firing of a weapon in a squad room. Perhaps they did not want to rock the boat at this time to prepare a case against me since we were all moving out soon. The Chief, of course, did not say anything and no one else did either. I was almost in shock realizing I could have killed a man.

The next day we were shipping out to advance training in North Carolina. I'm sure the officers had an idea about what had happened although everyone kept silent. Chief never gave me an accusing look or a word of disapproval.

After we shipped out, I never saw Chief again.

◆   ◆   ◆

Krup, Long, LaForse and I were ordered to report to New River, North Carolina for advanced training. Probably because of the alphabet we continued to be assigned the same details. It was the end of October of 1944 and our short guard duty tour at Boston Navy Yard became memories.

Lafarge had not been far from his home in New Hampshire and was able to get to see his family on some long liberties that he arranged for himself with poker winnings. Several times he was listed as AWOL but somehow managed to get back into base without penalty.

Krup spent every hour that he could being with Wanda and planning their future after the war. He enjoyed her family and got to know them very well. They were pleased with the choice of husband that their daughter had made and took Dan into their family quickly and with much affection. The couple was in love and each day that separated them was painful.

Long fell in love during every other liberty and he had a big group of girls to write to in addition to his girl in Philly, Deirdre. It would keep him busy for the days ahead until he decided he loved only Deirdre and then she was all he talked about.

Although we never met, Wanda and Deirdre, became very well known to us after hearing Krup and Long talk about them, seeing their photos, and listening to their letters being read. Of course, whenever they wrote to the girls they mentioned us, and the girls got to know us too. Phyllis and I wrote a couple of letters to each other, found little in common to talk about, and then we were absorbed into separate worlds we were never meant to share. I wondered over the years if she remembered how young we were while we shared a few hours during World War ll.

◆   ◆   ◆

New River, Camp LeJuene, North Carolina

Thousand of us were being trained for the coming battles in the Pacific. If we were lucky we would be able to land on Iwo or Okinawa before the war was over and not miss the big show. We lived in an enormous city of green, eight man tents that sprawled across the scrub pines of North Carolina. They called it tent city. We learned how to bayonet, strangle, and kill an enemy in many ways.

We threw hand grenades that were live. We crawled under live machine gun fire. Practiced bayoneting stuffed enemies and yelling, "Die Dirty Jap", and fired on obstacle courses with spring up targets. We went on long marches without enough food and water just to toughen up. It was war games time again, but without the Drill Instructor harassment.

It got so cold in the tents during the November and December of 1944 that the frost would build up inside and you could scrape it off with your knife in handfuls. We did this and made snowballs to throw at each other. We had little stoves burning kerosene for heat, and when the wicks went out and smoldered, black smoke filled the tent. Our faces would turn black from the smoke except for the white around the eyes that had been closed. We all looked like black faced comics as we came out of our tents in the early morning.

The cold was so severe, especially in the tents with the defective heaters, that in the morning we ran to dress in the heated, barrack type building that had the toilets and wash basins. We shaved, brushed our teeth, did the most personal things all in common view of our buddies. The large room smelled of urine. Men defecated while sitting over a long trough with running water splashing under them. Acqua Velva after-shave lotion odors mingled with the steam from the hot water showers and sinks. The lack of privacy was soon forgotten.

The food featured quantity rather than quality with plenty of grease to keep our stomachs alive and burning. Sometimes we got pork chops for several days in a row for breakfast, lunch and dinner. We suspected some local pig farmer of having a connection with the cooks.

As we ate in the mess hall at times the prisoners from the brig would be marched in for their meals. They had the letter P marked in white on all their pants and jackets and their heads shaved. As they marched in, the Marine MPs would whack them across the legs with a long baton just to keep them moving fast and torment them.

This was a tough brig, not like the one in Boston Navy Yard. I promised myself not to screw up here if I could help it.

The prisoners were a sad looking bunch of young men who had disobeyed a variety of rules, but the most frequent one was going AWOL.

The MPs shouted at them as they ate, for no reason other than to remind us onlookers what would happen if we screwed up. Witnessing the treatment of those prisoners served as a lesson to all of us to keep our noses clean. They ate their meals in fifteen minutes or less. When they left they stood at attention, arms folded across their chest and touching the back of man in front of them. In this manner they marched out of the mess hall in lock step.

The brig was located in the center of the tent city so that we could witness how the prisoners were being treated. The brig area was surrounded by a electrified, barbed wire fence and we could see much of activity when we passed. The prisoners lived in tents too but they had no cots. At times their sleeping area would be hosed down with water to make them more miserable in that cold autumn.

The treatment at this brig was cruel and constant. Never did we see the prisoners relaxing. When they were marched outside the stockade they were shouted at and sworn at and constantly banged across their shins with those long batons. We hated to see men treated that way, especially fellow Marines. It was difficult to accept the fact that Americans would treat other Americans that way.

No one in this brig was going to sneak in bits of food for his friend. This was one of the toughest brigs in the country. I guess the one next in order of severity would be the Navy brig in Portsmouth, New Hampshire, legendary in the Marines and the Navy for its toughness.

Although I feared that brig I chanced a few escapades just to survive at a higher standard.

There seemed to be a shortage of everything in New River. Sometime we needed a hat or pair of boots or jacket. The only thing you could do was requisition something for yourself if you wanted it. The Marines were great for requisitioning. Unofficially the Corps condoned it without argument. If you needed something you did not have you were expected to supply yourself the best you could. I had a little training in that respect in civilian life.

I felt sorry for the other kids I met in the Corps who had come from regular families that had food on the table every day and had fathers and mothers at home to wash their shirts and give them money to spend for the movies. I never had that and had to scrounge for myself and knew how to requisition very well.

Many of the boys from the Midwest were also very religious and would not break any commandments. They found the Corps a tougher place than others. You had to take care of yourself very often until the military bureaucracy could provide for you.

I felt sorry for the Bible Belt kids too who had a very religious bringing up. Here they were subjected to every curse word and blasphemy that the human mind could conjure. The name of God and Jesus, all the angels and saints were constantly used in degrading fashion and the good Christians would cringe.

I had grown up during The Depression in a broken home mostly unsupervised by my father who was busy keeping things together. I'd stolen food from stores, pilfered clotheslines at night to get a shirt to wear to school, stolen coins from various areas to attend a movie or buy an ice cream soda. Now I had a lot of these things, including good food, given me, free movies, and even got paid for it. However, at times there were shortages.

If the Corps did not issue a piece of equipment, I had no problem in supplying myself.. The Corps was my type of place in this regard. I and my buddies profited by having that extra tub of ice cream, newer boots, and various other small luxuries which I requisitioned.

On a higher level, if a Marine unit did not have a piece of equipment, it would be requisitioned from the Navy or the Seabees or wherever it was available. Almost every military branch had more issued to them than the Marines who had to travel light, fast and hungry. The Navy, Seabees and Air Force had gourmet food compared to the Marines and at every opportunity we tried to eat at their mess halls. It was like being on special liberty for us. Once we were in a Seabee mess hall and noticed that the chow line was unmanned and unguarded. You could help yourself to as much as you wanted. We found that unbelievable.

Nothing of value was ever left unguarded in the Marines and I understood this very well. I knew the value of things that I had so little of. When they placed me on mess duty as a punishment for some insubordination they made a big mistake. I and my buddies would be supplied with the best of the food available via the back door.

Once I had to explain my possession of new boots which had not been officially issued as yet.

"Where did you get these boots, Private?"

"Requisitioned sir."

The officer smiled knowingly. He was not a tight ass who did things by the book. There were a few officers who were that way, but most protected their little privileges of special food, clothing, and whiskey rations. However, at times, they too enjoyed requisitioned extras.

If you complained that you did not have something you were likely to be greeted with the response, "Semper Fi", a shortening of Semper Fidelis, from another Marine. This meant "tough shit", or "Hooray for me and screw you!"

Being irreverent was often typical Marine behavior, especially during times of stress.

Respect for authority was difficult for me to handle too. I devised ways to avoid saluting officers by changing my direction when I spotted one approaching in the distance, or pretending not to see them when they passed. I was not exactly the man you wanted in your outfit if you were an officer. I was trouble and it was probably noted in my records which followed me to the next commanding officer who had the misfortune to inherited me. It was my letter A for asshole.

I got into the habit during this period of stealing a few bucks from my buddies who came back from their liberties drunk and broke, but this was not for personal gain. I knew we would like to see some of the sights in California when we got there and you needed a little money for that. I reserved a little nest egg for them. I had some of my own money which I guarded closely but they didn't guard theirs, especially LaFoo. He spent money foolishly or lost it. Although he would win at poker games at times, the money never remained in his pockets.

When we were ready for liberty and they had no money, I would surprise them by pulling out a roll of bills and told them where it came from. At first they were surprised and then angry and then soon forgot when we were all at the Hollywood Canteen, the Palladium, and other places that required a few bucks.

After New River's eight weeks of uncomfortable and depressing duty we packed into a long, rusty train that took us across America. An adventure of five days crossing the country followed, including almost an entire day for Texas. I never thought a state could be so big. On longer stops at train stations we fell out and trooped and drilled for exercise, and to entertain the civilians. Then finally we went into the beautiful sunshine of California.

California was a wonderland. The Marine base at Camp Pendleton with its pastel colors and the palms, the bright clear sky, the many flowers all lifted our spirits. It was a few days of heaven with no training or guard duty before we were packed aboard a little ship called the Sea Bass which squatted sullenly at the pier in San Diego. We climbed like a row of ants up the gangplank carrying our sea bags and back packs on our shoulders.

No bands played, no speeches were given, and only a few girls could be seen in the distance wearing brightly colored dresses on their way to work. They caught the eyes of many Marines who began to howl and scream like a pack of reindeer in heat. The girls ignored us and didn't even wave to their heroes who were saving them from the raping Japanese.

We entered in to the black hold of the Sea Bass leaving the pastel colors of San Diego quickly behind. The image of three young girls dressed in bright colors became quickly a part of our memory.

Packed five and six deep in the hold during the three weeks of our crossing, we vomited and farted during the early bad weather, sending up a stench of pure rot. This stench mingled with that of perspiration and food cooking in the mess, was conducive to sea sickness. If you could make it, you would carry your sea sickness topside and to the head where the floors, toilets and urinals were awash with vomit. Men rolled about in the gangways with the sickness wishing to die. I was one of them and knew the feeling.

At night we tried to sleep in our narrow beds which were sheets of canvas strung tautly on steel frames, twelve inches apart and twelve inches deep. Fully dressed. we climbed into it, the man above was about twelve inches or less away from your face depending how heavy he was, and the man below about the same distance beneath. Thousands of us were packed in like this and I felt a wave of claustrophobia wash over me but fought it off.

It took twenty one days to cross the Pacific in the little, fat Sea Bass which was not escorted, supposedly because she could outrun Japanese submarines. My bunk was next to the steel plates that were riveted together to make the hull of the ship. At night I would reach out and touch the sweating steel plates, and could see the rivets that tacked them together. I could feel the vibration of the engines passing through the plates, and the pounding of the waves against them. The whole Pacific Ocean was an inch of steel away.

Some of the days were spent pleasantly on deck where we read, smoked and watched the flying fish, green, white and blue, fly and swim along with the ship as it splashed its way across the Pacific leaving a smooth wake aft. At night we would be entertained by the sunsets that would set the horizon afire with combinations of colors that I had never seen before. Whiskers of clouds thousands of miles long intertwined in sheets of gold, scarlet, and purple. Rays of sunlight shooting up from the sun as it dipped into the horizon like a huge, burning wafer, flinging shafts of golden fire into the sky as the earth turned to end another day. My eighteen years had not seen sunsets like that.

I would read to myself from Rudyard Kipling, "On the road to Mandalay where the flying fishes play, and the dawn comes up like thunder out of China across the bay."

Oh, my God, I loved that part of it at eighteen. Looking out over the endless expanse of the Pacific and reading Kipling made me feel that big things were happening in my life, and bigger things were to come.

Crossing the equator was reason for celebration and initiation. sailors who had crossed previously looked forward to this event which gave them an opportunity to initiate Marines who hadn't. We were called 'pollywogs' by the sailors and initiated into the realm of "King Neptune". We were tied to long ropes and dunked into the ocean as the Sea Bass slowed for this activity. Then they painted our bodies in various colors of dye, shaved our heads and cracked raw eggs on them. Some of us were stripped to their underwear and wrapped in sheets and sprayed with water hoses until we fell on the deck.

After the initiation we were issued a small card indicating that we had crossed the equator on the USS Sea Bass on December 24, 1944 we had become 'the sons of Neptune'. The next day was the first Christmas we had ever been away from home. The next time we crossed the equator we were 'old salts' going north to Okinawa and there was no reason for initiation.

We had been aboard the Sea Bass about three weeks and knew that we would be close to land soon. We had all heard of Guadalcanal from newspapers, books, radio and movies. Especially the movies. I couldn't believe that I was going to see Guadalcanal when I had just seen the movie only a few months ago. That is the way the government planned it, propaganda movie and then the real thing.

The movies had brought the war home to us young kids who were ready for adventure of any kind. Generations of young men are always ordered to serve the military programs that nations put together. In this war, Hollywood and the young generation that would fight it grew up together. Soon after a battle was fought, Hollywood would have it's version of it on the screen for the country to watch. Everybody was a hero, and more enemy died than Americans. Hollywood depicted a sanitized and romantic war where no one died anonymously.

During our last days on the Sea Bass we eagerly anticipated landing on the historical island that the Marines transformed into a shrine. Someone had a map of the South Pacific and located Guadalcanal on it for all of us to see where it was. So small, it was such a tiny place, just a stones throw from the enormous land mass of Australia. But it was still the Canal and it was surrounded by islands whose names were recently added to legends of Marine history; New Guinea, Savo, Tulagi, New Caledonia were all on that map and we would be there soon.

3

Training, Guadalcanal

This is the Island steeped in Marine Corps legend of bravery and courage. Marines who died here are remembered at bases throughout the country. They turned the tide of war. An inscription on a painting depicting Marines in battle.

In a short eight months our group of young kids had gone through Boot Camp, served guard duty at Boston Navy Yard, completed training at New River, crossed the country by train and the Pacific by boat. We had not traveled more than fifty miles from home before that. The adventures were coming quickly in our lives, and we were eager for more.

One misty, humid morning in January 1945 the Sea Bass slowed its speed and took on a pilot who would took us into the harbor. You could see the greenery of the island in the distance. The jungle had that deep green that almost turned black with its denseness. Other colors, when they appeared, seemed painted on the green. A palm tree here and there, another slim and yellowish, a golden beach like a slash of paint just before the jungle begins again. But it is the deep, solid green that dominates the eye as the ship eases into port.

I thought of the Tarzan movies and Africa. Again, Hollywood and the movies being the reference point in my young and unsophisticated world. Apes should be coming out of that jungle at any time now. The Tarzan movies had jungle scenery like this. It was so real and vivid, that it seemed unreal.

It was so absolutely exciting and adventurous. I wondered what other excitement would life be bringing us in the days ahead. Most of the islands in the Pacific had been fought for and won. Here at the bottom of the Pacific, if you looked on the map, there was little else to be fighting for. The battles of Saipan, Tinian, Guam, all the way up the Pacific, these battles were over. There was only scuttlebutt about places called Iwo Jima and Okinawa. They would offer young men the greatest adventure in their lives, and perhaps their time to die.

To Marines at that time, Guadalcanal was sacred ground. A place where so many of its men fought and died in the jungle when the war was being lost. This was a legendary island where men performed remarkable deeds that entered the lore of the Corps. Ordinary men who became heroes, walked, bled and died on this jungle floor. Marine conversation all across the Pacific included the Canal, and the word seeped into the stories told at night at Boot Camps in Parris Island and San Diego.

There was the man who held off hordes of enemy with a machine gun for many hours, the man who fired mortar shells by himself after his men were killed. Men who died obeying orders when there was no place else to go. Looking out to the Coral Sea you knew that underneath those waters were thousands of men of both sides who went down with their ships, and in doing so, left legends of heroism and pain. I wish they were here.

The museums in Quantico, Parris Island and San Diego contained the records of those events. Naval museums also exist in Yokahama and Tokyo telling their view of the story.

We knew the names of those who won their medals here in this rotting swamp of a place that harbored microbes, spoors, virus and fungus for eons. It was a land that fed on itself and defecated its own garbage and slime. Its humidity was held close to its dense jungle growth and did not permit evaporation. Our skin became infected with fungus and spores we called jungle rot because we were never dry.

The jungle was reclaiming its territory as it spread over tanks, guns and planes that were discarded or destroyed here. Soon the evidence of war and its heroes would be gone and the Lever Corporation of Britain would return to harvest coconuts to make soap products with the labor of a people not far from the stone age. These Solomon Islands natives often visited our camps, half cloth and bare footed, to sell sea shells they had fashioned into jewelry.

During training marches into this maze of jungle vegetation we were confronted by walls of growth that seemed miles high and endlessly deep that cast off a fog of humidity that clogged in our lungs. Then as we made our way by cutting through some of this lush growth we entered a clearing that had no tree cover and permitted the sun to burn into our bodies unfiltered by the tree top shade. The sun felt like it was sitting a mile over our heads, frying us as it sucked up all the juices from the jungle and other bodies.

We fell out for a rest and someone found a stream that has revealed itself by its loud gurgling against slippery rocks that had probably been there when the volcanoes first erupted to create this place.

"Water, there's water over here."

Can you imagine what this meant to us in that blistering heat with only a half filled canteen of piss warm water to drink?

Water, water, water. It ran down from the mountains that we could not see because the jungle grew too close to us even in the clearing. It ran down in large waves of splashing froth, dashing against the stones and dead trees forming a pool of clear liquid that men could swim in, and then spilled over and continued to the ocean.

Never, never in our lives had we ever felt water that cold. Whether it was because of our heated condition and the long trek through the jungle or that the water was formed from some magical, icy place in mountains, we did not know. The cold sting of it reversed the cruel, magnified heat of the sun and we frolicked like children half naked and happy on the Canal in January 1945. We were warned not to drink it because hidden in its sparkle, and sterling appearance, could be invisible bacteria that destroys human tissue. But we swallowed a mouthful or two anyway.

We lived on the beach sand in rows of neat tents and we decorated the tent rows with borders of sea shells and coconuts to identify walks and roads. Chunks of coral were place artistically about the area near the white Lister bags that held purified drinking water. They glowed like ghosts on a moonlit night suspended underneath wooden canopied shelters. After a cool jungle evening, rivulets of condensed water ran down the outside of the bags as the water inside began to warm under the relentless tropical sun.

Each of the green tents had canvas cots covered with mosquito netting. Militarily clean and orderly, equipment and uniforms, rifles and sea bags were each assigned a location in the tent and occupied it as ordered. Each tent repeated the image of its neighbor. There was no room for nonconformity here and in that respect I did not mind conformity. Individualism in living areas leads to chaos.

The creative use of sea shells and coconut husks decorated the borders along the tent rows, a playful deviation permitted from the functional, military way of things.

The ordered discipline, the rows of shells and coconuts, the green tents stretched militarily taunt and correct, the Lister bags, clean, white and reassuring with their contents of drinkable water, and the palm trees at attention, except for a few with congenital malformation and slanted, at ease in the wind, assured us that all was right in our world.

Even the orders to take malaria preventative Atabrine tablets everyday under strict supervision was a comforting discipline. The Corps was taking care of us. It had a big investment in us. There was important work they had for us to do.

The Atabrine pills were yellowing our skin after a few weeks and there was some controversy as to their possible side effects other than skin yellowing. We taunted each other saying, "you are beginning to look like a Jap," as we tanned, yellowed and grew long whiskers on our faces. We knew that Quinine had been replaced by this new skin-yellowing drug and the malaria cases were reduced considerably. Some of the Guadalcanal veterans who had caught malaria shivered and sweated in their bunks during sieges of the disease. Atabrine was not available to them during their time there.

It was a great adventure to be young, healthy and a Marine on Guadalcanal, which on the map seems to be floating like a little piece of shit north of Australia. (Look at the map of the South Pacific and see for yourself.) In civilian life my big trip was taking the number 44 bus from Lodi to Passaic, a trip of five miles, past rows of textile and rubber factories and small dilapidated store fronts nailed with "For Rent" signs. It was an ugly and depressing five mile journey I repeated many times during The Depression.

Order, romance, youth, good health and pride of service exhilarate us and made us feel invincible. Being young with many pages of our lives to be written, we eagerly welcomed each day. Each day was one of expectation. If they were boring you knew that they would be changing soon to surprise you.

We were slim, muscular, tanned, young and handsome in our faded dungarees, bleached almost white by the salt water and the sun. Those photographs that recorded our existence then are still kept in family albums and consulted from time to time to corroborate our memories.

At this point I did not envy my younger friends who were still in school and would be too young for this war. For my age group it was our last chance to be in this war. A war like this could never happen again. If it did it would really be the one to end all wars and perhaps the world too. But already governments were planning the possibilities.

Returning to our tent after a training session we saw a Marine putting his gear in place around the empty cot that that had been awaiting an occupant. New men were joining our units every day to build us into combat strength. The logistics experts were reaching all over the Pacific and the States for men. They were rushing recruits out of Boot Camp and sending them overseas without further training and lowering the training standards to meet quotas.

The man facing me seemed older than the usual recruit replacement. He was an odd sort of guy with a big head, thick glasses and closely cut hair. His thick shoulders and sturdy frame told you that he was familiar with hard work or sports. He was adjusting the mosquito netting in the cot next to mine.

When I came in the tent he looked around and said, "Hi, my name is Karnes, Lee."

"They call me Lance," I told him.

From his manner I knew immediately that we were compatible. He soon entered into our daily routines and we became friends. Over the next few days I learned that Lee had been side tracked for medical reasons while the doctors checked out his eye sight. They designated him 4F, physically unfit for duty. Lee fought to change that classification for patriotism and egotism. He wanted to be in the war particularly because he wanted to prove that he could physically do it, and because he was a Jew.

Born in the Williamsburg section of Brooklyn, he was an Hasidic Jew. He described them to me as guys who wear beards and long hair that they tuck behind their ears, yarmulkes and are always praying for mankind and peace. He told me about the prayer rituals and the various objects used as they prayed like leather straps and boxes. It all sounded so foreign to me, and Lee was at a point where he had doubts about religion in general.

I was anti-Semitic for two reasons in my young life before I met Lee. During Catechism lessons the nuns told us that the Jew killed Christ and made all the kids angry with Jews. After Catechism we would leave on a crusade looking for Jews to punish, but found none. I only knew one Jewish kid and he allowed me to play with his toys. I remembered that he always had a large chocolate cake to eat that sat on top of his refrigerator. He never offered me a piece. I resented that, and became anti-Semitic without knowing it for that reason, too.

When I told Lee, he laughed.

"I've heard a lot of reasons for being anti-Semitic but never that," he said.

He kept a low profile and was irritated whenever I did something that drew attention to us. He felt being a Jew had given him issues to deal with that he did not want to face in the Marines. He didn't go around telling everyone he was a Jew, but he told me soon after we met and we talked about poetry and God.

What problem could he start by being a Jew? I had not read much history at that time. Later I learned how much damage anti-Semitism had done in the world and how many people were murdered because of it. I wondered if it was because of the Catechism and chocolate cake. You know, in a way it was.

◆   ◆   ◆

Our tent rows were only fifty yards from the rusting, red, hulk of a beached Japanese troopship that had been bombed during the battle for the island. Her prow was lifted high out of the water and she looked like she was gasping for air and trying to free herself from the coral that was already beginning to grow around her. In time she would become a permanent thing of the sea. Part ship, part coral.

Half of her was in the sand where she had beached. Red rust flakes like fish scales were peeling from her plates and dropping into the sea. The rivets that held her hull together were beginning to pull away as the steel oxidized and warped.

When we swam out to her we looked up and saw her name painted on the prow, *Kinugawa Maru.*

Hundreds of young Japanese died in her belly as she beached herself in November 15, 1942 trying desperately to escape the American bombs and deposit her human cargo on the shore. She was a reminder of the fury that was typical on this island and this sea just a few months ago.

We started a ritual in those days on the Canal when we would swim out to the ship at the end of the day. With a short swim we were able to reach her and touch the rusting plates as the soft, salt water of the South Pacific lapped against her, deteriorating her with every lick of a wave. If we tired of swimming, there were parts of her that we could hold on to and rest. She was a wounded thing to me and I felt this sad boat and I had something in common.

The war was still on, so some were proud of the victory that destroyed her and her cargo, but I also sensed the sadness in her as she rusted in her grave. Her sister ships and many of our own ships that were destroyed in that battle, lay at rest, swallowed by the deeper waters of this Coral Sea, but she, half submerged, remained in agony.

As we swam about her, feeling her steel flanks with our fingers, the scaling rust, the rivets holding the plates, the many shell holes, we found a particularly large hole that smashed her steel plates inward with a furious impact that left a twisted gnarl of steel as it entered her guts. It was a large opening which a man could swim through and enter the inside of the ship.

As the waves sloshed against her the water line rose and fell, and when it fell you could better see the opening and an eerie light that came from inside the hull. The light source was the sunlight entering the bomb holes in the steel plates of her deck. The shafts of sunlight filtered down to the water and oil that washed inside her. As the water swayed with the motion of the sea the colors would change.

Her color reflections lured us, as shiny objects lure children. We challenged each other who would be the first to swim into the Maru where so many men had died? You could still smell diesel oil that bled from her engines emitting rainbow slicks on the blue waters.

Krup and LaFoo were the first to dive into the Maru and they described the interior.

"You can hear echoes all over the ship", they said, "lights all over the place and creaking sounds."

Long was next to enter the ship and then came out and entered her again. He had no problem with the venture and laughed and smiled with each dive. A group of other Marines also dared the dive into the Maru.

"Come on Lance don't be chicken, its easy. Hey, guys Lance is chicken," they taunted me.

Then they climbed on top of ship and walked to the higher section where they could dive off into the water. Some just sprawled on the rusty plates to sun bath. Whether I swam into the ship or not was not really important to them, but it had become very important to me.

These braver men than I had made the dive into the Maru. I hated myself for my fear. How could I pretend to love adventure and not know how it felt to swim into her?

I told Lee about my problem and he reassured me that it was not a big deal, and promised to swim out to the ship with me the next time and he did.

We swam out together one afternoon and each time I swam out to her I would examine the shell hole in her side and planned what had to be done.

"You go from air to water and to air again inside the ship", Lee said. "When you come up inside the ship there will be air for you to breath."

Then Lee reminded me of the scene in *Martin Eden*, Jack London's book. The character wants to commit suicide by drowning but when he dives he reserves enough air to rescue himself and returns to the surface of the water.

"It's the same thing, Lance," he said. Only you have enough air to come up inside the ship where there is air again."

I dove deeply and began to hear the voices of the dead Japanese soldiers, I could see them as skeletons waiting for me, I could hear the sounds of the battle that had destroyed them and I turned back toward the surface where it was safe. I had saved enough oxygen to go inside but did not do it.

"It takes a little time, Lance," Karnes said, and then told me how Eden had resolved his own problem.

"He dove deep and fast using all his oxygen going down, then when he changed his mind and tried to regain the surface, it was too late. All his oxygen was gone, he could not come up again. He drowned.

"Thanks," I said, and Karnes laughed.

Then I noticed that Karnes did not attempt to dive into the Maru, and it was not like him to be giving advice on something and not do it himself. I asked him why?

"Oh," he said "I have no interest in doing that. It's just a game and not important."

That made me feel a little better but I still felt lacking for not following the rest of the guys. It was the old teenage challenge to follow the leader. I could see then that Lee knew who he was better than I knew myself. He had no urgency to do something based on the evaluations of others.

Our days on the Canal were ending. The Maru was a vanishing memory that I would recall in dreams many times as my own measure of failed courage.

We were busy with preparations for leaving the Canal, and finally boarded a large transport that took us up the Pacific to the atoll of Ulithi which was suitable for mooring ships and transferring personnel. We transferred to a LST (Landing Ship, Tank). This was a squat vessel, flat bottomed, and not very fast. It carried several smaller craft, amtracks, in her hold which we would board when landing on this island called Okinawa. The amtracks were built to operate on land and water.

The large transport steamed into the Ulithi on a windy day with choppy waves lifting it high up and down in the water. We were fed steak and eggs for breakfast and we knew that we were being prepared for a special assignment. Steak and eggs breakfasts always meant things were going to be rough that day. It was a dying man's meal.

We were ordered to climb down the rope netting hanging over the side of the transport thirty or forty feet from the water onto the deck of an LST. Saddled with full packs, and carrying our rifles and ammunition, we found the maneuver very difficult. This was the first time we had done it at sea from a bouncing transport to a wave tossed LST.

There was little room for error here and you either made it or you didn't. A few men slipped and fell into the LST or the water and where severally injured, and many of us lost our the steak and eggs into the sea before we were all aboard.

We lived on the deck of the LST for several days sheltered by a makeshift canvas cover from the sun and rain, as it made its way up the Pacific. We were on our final leg to Okinawa along with thousands of other crafts of all sizes from all over the Pacific. Our days were spent reading, chatting, complaining, playing cards and privately praying. Some cleaned rifles over and over, and others sharpened their bayonets and knives.

War games, guard duty and training were all things of the past. The reason for our existence was just up the Pacific a few days away at this place called Okinawa.

A Marine near me had a five cent White Owl cigar still in good condition, but a little frayed. I was in the mood to play a game with him.

"I'll give you five bucks for that cigar," I told the guy and he looked at me like I was nuts.

"It's only a five cent cigar," he said.

"I know," I said, "but I'll give you five bucks for it."

In our precarious situation I knew that five dollars would soon not be of any use to us. I had accepted the idea of forgetting the cost material things when faced with possibility of entering eternity very soon. It was the last money I had on me and knew there would be no place to spend it where we were going.

We made the deal and I smoked two puffs of that very bad cigar before throwing it away.

The guy with the five bucks realized suddenly the worthlessness of money in our situation and wanted to give the money back to me. I refused and he resignedly put it in his pocket.

I don't know what the he did with the five bucks or if he ever got to spend it. He'd have to go through three months on Okinawa first before money became a thing of value again. For my five bucks I got a memory of a lifetime but never bought a five dollar cigar again.

Each day we sailed closer to our target island. Our days filled with boredom and the private anticipation of what the battle would bring. We all had seen enough movies and training films to know that the next big scene would be a landing and then casualties and possible death.

JD spent much of the time on the LST cleaning his equipment and making sure all his gear looked top shape. You'd think that he was going to a parade. The rest of us prepared to a lesser degree being satisfied with just passing inspections.

LaFoo, silent as always, quietly oiled his rifle and sharpened his knives and bayonet until he found a poker game. Krup wrote letters to Wanda everyday. He propped her photo up on his cot and looked at it every time he stopped writing as though seeking inspiration from the pretty blond in the photograph.

The LST was full of card games of all types, but mostly poker, and some dice games. Some men played the game of pitching coins against a wall to see which one would land closest to it and become a winner. Arguments filled the air when rules were disputed and distances measured. Physical challenges were made when disputes got out of hand but the rest of us just laughed the would combatants into a truce. They realized the ridiculousness of their actions especially under those conditions and smiled sheepishly. It was a familiar Marine atmosphere we were accustomed to.

All of us wrote letters home where our thoughts and hearts were most of the waking hours. We wondered if those so far away were thinking of us.

In one letter I tried to get past the censors I mention that I had just been reading Richard Tregaskis, hoping that my friends got the hint. Tregaskis wrote *Guadalcanal Diary* and it was very popular at the time. It escaped the censor and my friend Billy knew where I was going.

4

Okinawa April 1, 1945

Our troops are under the fire of heavier artillery than has been encountered on any other island in the Pacific War. This campaign will see a lot of American dead and wounded before it ends. NY Times 1945.

It is Easter Sunday, April Fool's Day, April 1, 1945.

The sun came up like a big, fire red, ball spilling hot gases from its rim for thousands of miles around the horizon. The sky was on fire. I associated that sun with the round red ball on the Japanese flag. We are in enemy waters and about to land on Japanese territory only three hundred and fifty miles from the main islands of Japan. This is the closest that we have been to the enemy homeland on foot. We are in his waters and approaching his soil.

Surrounding us wherever we look are low slung battleships, destroyers and other ships of all sizes firing their guns broadside into the land that lies before us strangely quiet. Newspapers reported that this was the largest armada of ships for an invasion in the Pacific, and they have been bombarding this island for days.

Sheets of rockets are unleashed into the air like swishing fireworks from platforms on rocket carrying ships. Rockets, rockets by the thousands were launched to land harmlessly in rice fields and mountainsides. Rockets that can't penetrate caves, dug deep in the hills and mountains without causing casualties.

A puff of smoke leaves the long cannon of a battleship in the distance, we see the smoke and flash immediately and then after a brief pause, the sound waves bring the thunder to our ears.

Swarms of our planes fly over the land dropping bombs and shooting rockets. We are happy with all the death directed against the enemy. The more they kill the less we have to face ourselves.

Kill the F—, kill the gook Fu—, F, no good F. gooks Bastards gooks Jap F—gooks. Kill the F—Gooks Japss. Kill the Dirty F—good Japs yellow Bastards.

63

FFFFFFFFFFFFFFFFFFFFFFFFFFFFFFFFFFFFFFFFFFFFFFFFFFFFFFFF
FFFFFFFF   JapsFFFFFFFFFFF   gookFFFFFFFFFFFFFFFgooks   japs   Japs
FFFFFFFF!
FFFFFFUUUUUCCCCKKKKKKIIIIIINNNNngggggJaps—
KILLLLLLLLLLLLLLLL-Kill them.

Jesus Christ, killll the Fuuccckkking. Japanese.

We cheer for our side. Happy Easter!

Overhead the kamikaze come flying in, getting closer and closer until they reached their target and blew themselves against the hulls and decks of ships. They fly with insane purpose to glory for Emperor and Japan, killing and maiming sailors who were doing all the fighting now as we sat in our little boats. The enemy was not interested in small, troop carriers at that time and we were spectators as the Navy fought to protect the battleships, carriers and other larger ships. The guns on our LST joins in the shooting as a enemy suicide plane approaches. You can sense the excitement and fear of the gunners as the kamikaze persist in flying through the hail of tracer bullets.

Over and over the kamikaze swarm in like malignant mosquitoes persistently on and on droning and unwavering towards their targets. They don't try to deviate or disguise their course. It is just a steady, rapid flight either from a great height down onto a deck, or a low approach along the water aiming at the hulls. Most are hit in flight before they reach their targets and burst into flames in the air and disintegrate. Some go down into the water wing tip first and then tumble over and over and vanish in the smoldering water.

As the attacks continue many sailors are stressed to exhaustion by the constant attack of suicide planes. The tension is so taunt that the high command stops announcing when the kamikaze are coming to reduce the suspense and incidents of combat fatigue. When they are actually seen in the air the men at the guns have enough time to shoot back.

We cheer when one is shot down and curse when one hits an American ship. It's like a game, a movie. We are spectators with nothing to do but watch the Navy ships bombard the island and fight off kamikaze.

A small plane suddenly appears in the sky flying slowly along the beach of the island. Many American ships start firing at it with antiaircraft guns in rapid fire. There is an enormous concentration of gun fire for such a small plane.

"Why is he flying so slow?", we ask each other. "What kind of plane is that? Why is he flying so low?"

It has pontoons and looks so incongruous as though sight seeing in that turmoil. What was his mission we don't know. Is it a enemy plane? Then in seems the entire Navy is firing at that little plane that is flying so ridiculously slow and low as though it were on an excursion over a peaceful island and not a landing operation.

The small plane burst into flame and the fuselage burned quickly like crepe paper, leaving its frame silhouetted black in the blue sky. The pilot fell to the sea with the burning plane. We can see his body falling with the flaming debris.

We on the deck of the LST witness this as though it were a movie, not believing reality. We began to cheer when the little plane burst into flames and falls. We are close enough now to see the water swallow the larger cinders and belch puffs of smoke and we cheer and cheer and cheer.

Then Lee said, "that looked like one of our own surveillance planes."

We all said, "you're nuts."

After a brief moment the PA system of the LST crackled on and announced, "That plane that was just shot down near the beach was one of our own."

Lee was right. Someone remembered it was April Fools Day, and said, "April fool!"

But it was not an April Fool joke.

"How did you know that was one ours?," we asked Karnes.

"It was only a guess," he said, "but I wondered why it had pontoons."

It was the first casualty we saw of the battle and it was a mistake, an error. A man was killed. The excited sailors had mistakenly shot down one of our own planes when it was so obvious that it was harmless. Many more mistake were in the offing.

"Holy shit." We heard someone say and then there was a brief silence. We had cheered for the wrong side. No one said anything. There was a sour feeling of tragic loss, but we had no time to nurse it.

The PA system snapped on again to tell us to prepare for loading on the amtracks below deck. The PA system was like a phantom director orchestrating our movements and explaining events as they occurred.

The water was littered with many smoking and burning American ships, and many ships were firing at attacking planes and at the landing beaches as we take a last look before we climb down the ladders to our amtracks.

The amtrack, a small vehicle with tractors, could navigate on the water as well on land. The belly of the LST was loaded with several amtracks two abreast and lined up in a row nose to tail. As we all boarded, the LST moved closer toward the beach and we waited in the dim light of her belly expecting to be hit by a Japanese bombs at any minute.

The water was alive with hundreds of LSTs carrying Marines to the beaches, but now we could not see them.

Finally the LST's engines stopped and her two large bow doors opened, letting in the bright sunshine. We could see the sky and the beach about a mile before us as we stood in full gear, shoulder to shoulder, in the amtracks. The amtracks' engines start and move towards the open doors following the one before it into the water. No one talks. No jokes, no comments at all. The amtracks move so painfully slow on the long trip to the beach.

When the last amtrack moved out of the LST, the LST reversed its engines and aimed its bow towards the deep water again. We understand the eagerness of it's skipper to increase his distance from the landing beaches where hell is expected to erupt as in most landings in the Pacific.

The amtrack is so slow moving. We are like sitting ducks. If the enemy artillery finds us. there is nothing we can do to defend ourselves. We use body motion urging the slow craft to move more quickly toward the shore so that we can leave. We are vulnerable in this slow moving, bathtub-like boat, bobbing on the waves and inching its way shoreward. It takes an eternity to get there and when the front ramp of the amtrack is cranked down we all rush into the shallow surf and charge towards the enemy with great relief to be free of the floating coffin.

The whole scene is one of tense excitement. The expected fury of our imaginations does not materialize, but still we pray for salvation and survival. We had been trained, and we had seen the movies, and knew what to expect. We waited for the charging hordes of the enemy, the machine gun fire and the bombs to repulse our attack. Nothing happened. There were no enemy on the beaches or beyond. They had entrenched themselves, for the most part, in enormous caves in the southern end of the island and planned to fight from there in the coming days.

The enormous naval guns, aircraft, and rocket boats had been sending tremendous explosives into the beach and beyond for days. Any enemy in that area would have been decimated, but no one was there. All this gunfire and bombing resulted in little damage to the enemy but terrified the natives, and dug large holes in the ground. Now that we had landed, we found no one to fight.

In my anxiety, I aimed at a small bush that could not hide anyone and fired my rifle at it very closely over someone's head.

"What the hell are you shooting at?" the man shouted.

"I thought I saw something," I answer.

"There's nobody there." he said, exasperated by my nervousness.

It was the first shot I fired in the battle. I just had to shoot at something to relieve the pressure. We had landed on a deserted beach but I still felt the enemy was around us like ghosts.

All that day we quickly walked forward without seeing an enemy soldier. We were startled when a old, native man climbed out of a hole with a sweet potato and offered it us as a gesture of peace. We thought it was a hand grenade and jumped away from him quickly. The man stood about four feet, nine inches, and from his weathered appearance looked like a gnome.

As I walked forward I counted the yards of territory that I was claiming for the United States of America. When that first day turned into night we had covered over ten miles and were three days in advance of the invasion schedule. You move fast when there is no enemy to argue with you.

We dug holes for the night, ate raw sweet potatoes and K rations, and watched as the black sky was streaked with the colors of tracer bullets, bursting bombs and rockets like a huge blackboard being scribbled upon with chalks of fire. But this was not our fight. The Air Force and the Navy were doing their type of fighting now from a distance.

We were up early and on our way to conquer more land for the US of A, and locate the elusive enemy. We turned north up the island looking for him and finding only an occasional sniper position which was quickly knocked out after they inflicted some casualties. When we passed the sniper lair still concealed, but not invisible, we saw our first enemy dead. A group of puppet like Asian kids, smooth shaven except for wisps of hair on chins and cheeks, their heads broken open by bullets exposing a gray puddle of brains that leaked down and smeared over their faces into their opened eyes.

Are these real people, I wondered? Can these be humans or play dolls lying in grotesque positions. I remembered seeing discarded dolls in my hometown with their heads cracked, eyes open, and their hair and limbs yanked out of position. These dead soldiers looked the same, but softer.

We were ordered to walk and climb over terrible terrain all day and into the night. Not being able to see more than a foot or so in front of us when night fell. We had to hold on the each other as we walked or climbed, holding on to field jackets, pieces of equipment and even a hand.

We did not dare to talk in normal voices, just whispers. We were not told what we were looking for in particular and it did not matter. We carried full packs and ammunition but little food. The regular food supply was to reach to us later the next day. We ate whatever we had stored in our packs. I had a compressed fruit bar and chunk of hard, non-melting chocolate.

We whispered to each other for support and direction. At times we automatically picked up a dropped ammunition canister or other equipment discarded by exhausted men who fell on the ground crying and whimpering from over exertion. We anticipated walking into an enemy ambush, but would never know it until it was too late.

We could not see the faces of the fallen men but whispered to them to be quiet until they could walk again.

We did not know if the enemy was around the next turn or behind a large rock, or mingling with us in our blind march over the mountains. It was possible for enemy soldiers to join our ranks and kill someone and then disappear into the darkness. The man we followed, or who followed us in the dark could have been an enemy soldier.

It was impossible to carry those who fell. I remembered the Drill Instructors on Parris Island on the parade fields shouting at us when a man fell while we were playing war games.

"March over him," they shouted, "step on him, don't stop marching. The meat wagon will pick him up."

There were no meat wagons up in those mountains that night, and you lay where you fell. No one stepped on you, but they could not stop and carry you either.

In the pitch darkness, you followed the man ahead of you blindly, being directed only by the pull from his jacket as you held on and he moved ahead holding on to the man ahead of him. It was one long dark line of men climbing over and around rocks, through bushes, and along steep ridges were the small stones rolled under your feet. Men lost their balance and fell moaning as they rolled away from the line and fell among the stones.

Most of us made it through that night into the next day. Some didn't. Some were injured physically and others mentally. We who made it felt physically superior to those who didn't. I was embarrassed for those who could not finish the march and knew that many others felt the same way too. We thought some were faking physical and mental exhaustion, but why would you do that when there was no place to seek refuge. I made it through that night, but my night was coming.

The April warmth and rain had encouraged the young plants to grow just like in Chaucer's Prologue of the *Canterbury Tales*.

"When April with its sweet showers had pierced the dry roots of March…and bathed each vine in sweet liquor,"

That spring on Okinawa the young carrots were showing their green shoots just above the soft dirt. If you dug into the dirt you could find a sweet potato, too.

We had walked through the night without eating and under extremely hard conditions carrying heavy gear ammunition and weapons. Our bodies were exhausted and our stomachs had that raw, empty pain of hunger. Perhaps corpsmen in the meat wagons in the rear had been picking up those who had fallen, but the food supply had not reached us by late morning. My concentrated fruit bar and hard chocolate were consumed. I had given the fruit bar to Krup who had no food in his pack and he protested but accepted it when his large frame ran out of energy. I ate the bitter chocolate bar.

Some had noticed the young carrot shoots and began digging them out of the ground with bayonets and K-bar knives, and wiping off the dirt on their jackets. No one wanted to waste canteen water to wash them. They had to collect a handful to make a satisfying mouthful and then ate green shoots, carrots and bits of dirt in satisfying gulps. We looked like animals scavenging in the dirt for handfuls of carrots.

Our young lieutenant tried to maintain his dignity did not join in the carrot orgy, but he did accept carrots from those who offered him some and ate with equal gusto.

I realized how quickly man can turn from human to beast without food to eat. Within several short hours the lack of food and water can drive a man to actions he did not contemplate and would embarrass him when remembered later. A few more days without food and we would be at each other's throats.

Patrols were organized to send us into enemy territory to draw fire or discover some information about the enemy's strength.. A patrol was a search operation that often did not have a specific goal other than to expose a group of men to enemy eye balls and gun fire and see what the reaction was and if resistance was heavy. During fierce combat conditions patrols were often illogically ordered and often disobeyed.

One night during heavy combat, JD, LaFoo and I were ordered to volunteer for a patrol that was to be led by a young replacement sergeant. We tried to talk the lieutenant out of the order telling him that there was too much fire. Mortar shells were dropping heavily but we were in the safety of a small cave and did not want to move out of it. The lieutenant decided that we would go on patrol and keep in touch with him by radio which were not very reliable at that time.

Cursing to ourselves, we left the cave and went into the rainy night three men led by a green non com. Occasional flares would turn night into weird daylight and we dropped to the ground for cover. We did not get more than a twenty five feet out of the cave when we found a group of large rocks among which we could take cover. We remained there for a while and then tried to contact the lieutenant in his cave.

The Japanese had a one man mortar called the knee mortar and it was considered very accurate. One of these mortar shells exploded inches from my foot and in a jerk reaction I kicked at it like it was an animal, and screamed at the same time. The mortar shell did no harm. Why? Who knows?

"We are pinned down out here, lieutenant and we can't go further," the sergeant exaggerated our condition a little because we had urged him to do so. He had been on line only a day or two and was ready to take his orders from us who had been there much longer.

The lieutenant ordered us to remain out for a while and see if we could locate any enemy. What he was doing was using us a bait for Japanese mortar and machine gun fire, and this did not seem fair to me.

The flares continued to turned night into that brief, false daylight so frequently that it was impossible to move for a distance without being exposed. More mortar rounds fell very close to our position indicating that the enemy knew where we were.

We contacted the lieutenant again and told him we were still pinned down and were coming back into the cave and he grudgingly agreed. We saved our own asses that night by not blindly following orders that were ill advised..

What the lieutenant reported to company, and company to battalion, I didn't know nor cared to know. How they record the action of that night in history, I don't care. I do know that those far behind the line, and those not too far behind, like the lieutenant in the cave, don't know what is going on at the front where the fighting is.

I was the one who suggested to giving the lieutenant the pinned down report, after I tried to kick away the mortar shell and screamed. Krup, LaForse and JD agreed that it was the right thing to do. The sergeant just had to go along with us. The only thing we would have accomplished that night was getting ourselves killed and becoming automatic heroes.

There was always an amount of apprehension when patrols were planned. The biggest concern was being chosen for the point position. That would be the first man to lead the patrol column into enemy territory and expose himself to their gun fire. It was not the worse position to be in physically because the enemy usually allowed the point man to enter deeply into the area and expose more of the patrol so that they could cut them in half and fire to the rear and the point at the same time.

Still, you never knew if some young enemy kid on seeing the point man, would shoot him first, forgetting the logic of letting the entire column get into range. Psychologically, being at the point was nerve wracking. You felt the eyes of the enemy on you even if they were not. You imagined the sights of the rifles were on you and that any moment they would be squeezing off a shot that would tear into your body. You anticipated the burn of the round in your back or belly, you knew if it hit your head you would not know the next second of life. You wondered how it would be in that time between being and not being. Any second could be your last.

◆   ◆   ◆

The Battalion had spent the night dug in at the edge of the sea. So beautiful, the wind swept shrubs and trees grew leaning towards the land and were silhouetted against the haze of the morning mist. Offshore were a few picturesque, stone outcroppings with a few trees growing on them like miniature islands in Oriental parchment paintings, delicate, sensitive, haunting. The golden sand and glistening water added further to this aura of peace.

The morning chow had been finished and the Battalion was falling into units that would participate in the patrol across a wide valley and into the mountains in the distance.

This was a big patrol with many men. Usually the other patrols were smaller with a squad or platoon participating, maybe fifteen to thirty men. Very often just four or five men would be sent out. But the procedure and the concerns were about the same.

The selection of position began. "Battalion, L Company, third platoon, third squad, third fire team, the choice had fallen down to me.

"Take the point, Poet," one of the company sergeants said. There was a note of happiness in voice that I resented but I could do nothing but accept it. I tried not to show my displeasure. Sergeants and I did not get along. I was carrying too many black marks in my military history.

I began walking out into the valley that stretched before us with high hills on either side and flat rice patties, now dry before the planting season, and dry enough to walk on with ease. The heavy rains had not come yet, but in a month the dirt would slide from under our boots and turn the area to chocolate pudding.

Krup was not far from me and shouted, "We're right behind you, Lance, don't worry."

From a distance I saw LaFoo who was in another platoon give me the thumbs up gesture.

JD was not far behind me and he knew how it felt to be at the point. He had been there himself on patrols and was not far from me now. They knew what was going through my mind.

I took little consolation from any sign of encouragement and looked up into the valley where on either side were heavy growth of trees, bushes and mounds of rocks where the enemy could see us coming. It was not a welcoming sight despite the bright sun shining and the cool breeze blowing at our backs from the sea.

I thought, "Into the valley of death, rode the six hundred." Tennyson, *The Light Brigade*. We weren't cavalry, so we walked into the valley. Would death be there to greet us? Yes, I was certain she would be waiting.

The enemy could see the column of Marines come toward them being led by a skinny, teenage boy who kept looking back over his shoulder at the following column as though he did not want to leave it too far behind. To them, I'm sure, I looked to be a very timid Marine.

Whenever I looked back to see how far ahead I was, an officer would wave at me to keep walking. I did not want to be too far ahead, but they wanted me way out there at the point alone where I belonged. I felt like I was miles ahead of them and it was so very lonely. When I looked back I could see a long single column of men following me but could not see the end of it. I kept on walking and looking into the hills and trees for signs of the enemy and saw nothing.

My purpose was not to locate the enemy necessarily, but to expose myself to him which I did very well. He knew we were there and just waited.

After walking for about an hour into the valley, suddenly the zinging of bullets and the cries of wounded men began to fill the air. As I fell to the ground I looked to the rear and could not see a single man. Everyone had hit the dirt and found the best cover he could. I was near a small brook bed that was dry, and the bottom was full of small, round stones. I rolled into it and began to dig away the stones to get deeper into the earth. On either side of the dry brook a mound of dirt helped to protected me from enemy fire. Several men were now in the gully with me and one had a BAR (Browning Automatic Rifle) but he wasn't shooting it, and I told him to shoot.

"I can't see anything to shoot at" he said.

I said, "Shoot the fucking thing at the bushes in the hill."

I don't know if he was afraid to give away his position or what. Some men carrying automatic weapons were reluctant to fire and expose themselves as important targets. I kept shooting my inconspicuous rifle at illusions in the far away hills perhaps hitting only some trees and stones.

More and more cries of wounded men continued. The firing was probably coming for the high ground to the left but I could not see a goddamn thing. I'm sure no one else did either. Someone ordered us to move out of the ditch and get into a position on the opposite high ground which was several hundred yards across the valley. As the men ran out of the ditch the ticking of bullets followed them kicking up puffs of dust at their heels. Real bullets, I thought, those are real bullets. The enemy could see us and we did not know where they were. We did not know how to protect ourselves from the bullets and where to shoot back.

When my turn came to run out of the ditch I expected the bullets to bite into my legs. Some kicked up the dirt along my feet and I began the long run across the rice patties into the opposite high ground with everyone else. We were all running. I'm sure everyone ran in fear, away from enemy fire and not towards him.

It was the longest, hardest, most brutal, fearsome run I had ever made in my life.

We ran in a zig zag manner to avoid the bullets and dared not to fall on the ground where we would be stationary targets. But the long run at maximum speed, carrying heavy equipment and ammunition, drained us and we fell to the ground in exhaustion, taking the chance of being an easier target.

When I fell to the ground, my lungs on fire and my muscles in pain, I looked into the dirt and a saw a yellow flower that looked familiar, like a butter cup. It had pushed itself up out of the earth in this remote rice field.. It was so incongruous growing there so far away from my childhood meadows of New Jersey where I used to pick them during grammar school field trips.

I turned my head without lifting it so that I could see the sky above me which was just perfect with white clouds and pale blue expanses.

"I wondered lonely as a cloud that floats on high over vale and hill and all at once..." Wordsworth., and there I was, waiting for the fire in my lungs to cool so that I could run again to save my life.

I held a handful of the dirt to my nose and smelled it. It looked dark and alive. This is what men die for, earth, dirt, inches of it, yards, and miles of it. Stretches of earth in the form of countries all over the world were fought for and I visualized the various armies and hoards that fought over the land since the beginning of whatever began.

This dirt witnessed our fighting, as dirt all over the world through the centuries witnessed battles and absorbed the blood of young men. I saw all the small, yellow flowers had been pushing themselves up out of the black earth where the sunlight caught them and transformed them into bright gold.

Wordsworth again, "…I saw a crowd, a host of golden daffodils."

Now around me the enemy bullets were kicking up bits of stone and earth. They had located us where we fell to rest. Men were crying and shouting all around in confusion. My body, heart and soul were engulfed in almost paralyzing fear and I pressed my face into the soft dirt trying to become one with it away from the screaming and pain.

A voice of authority, tinged with panic, shouted, "let's move."

I got up and ran until the fire in my lungs returned and almost burn through my chest. The humid air I sucked into my scaring lungs became hot steam and then dried. As I ran I lost my rifle sling, my helmet fell off my head. My back pack felt like a load of lead and my canteen bounced and slapped wildly against my thigh and hip. I wanted to rid myself of everything so that I could move faster, even my rifle, but remembered it was my best friend.

My best friend was very heavy and of little help that day.

Finally we reached the higher ground across the valley where there was shelter and cover among the brush and trees. Who had chosen that location to run to? I don't know, but that is where we ran like wild things chased by death.

When we had regrouped and the officers in charge realized what had happened, we started our long retreat back to the beach where we had started the patrol that morning.

We had been ambushed and forced to retreat under fire we could not see. You couldn't see a single enemy soldier. When we reached the rear position several jeeps loaded with dead Marines in contorted positions were already there. No one spoke and we just sat there smoking. cigarettes. One jeep had a short wave radio that was getting news.

President Roosevelt had died. No one said anything about that but Karnes, who recalled the President's social programs that had help so many poor people.

"He was a good man," Karnes said.

Most of us did not know or care about that.

The jeeps with the dead Marines were parked in front of us, and someone covered the bodies with a poncho. We had no sadness for the President then. We were mourning our young friends who had just died a few minutes ago. These young boys piled in the jeeps lost all the days of their lives and we could have been alongside them. The President was an old man and had lived his days. That's how we measured things, not by social status or historical worth.

It was April 12, 1945. Few would ever know about those dead young men in the jeeps, except their families, while the death of the President would be recalled for a long time along with his speech indicating, "December 7, 1941, a day that will live in infamy."

Not one enemy soldier was killed as far as we knew, but we had located his position and served our purpose. The area would soon be hit with artillery and air bombardment and then we would try to cross the valley again. Over and over and over. Eventually all that dirt we retreated over would be ours.

That day made me aware of the sudden finality of death. It could come at any time quickly without warning. You could be, for one moment, and then, not be, for eternity. It was no complicated thing. No big deal. It was a simple passage we all would eventually make. Your body would no longer respond to the last command from your brain. You were dead.

◆   ◆   ◆

Was war always like this? Did the earth bring forth beautiful flowers and the sky turn blue and soft while men killed each other amidst such exquisite beauty? Did they bleed into that earth of their time, shit into it, pissed into it while the butter cups and all living things insisted on continuing the cycle of the universe? Do only poets wonder about this?

All these wars stretch out far behind us and we erect monuments to remember and dedicate holidays to pay tribute. There are so many to remember that we group them into one. Memorial Day, a big, fussy day for remembering so much disaster. As we speak another is in progress and we participate in it each evening on our television screens. And all the other countries of the world do the same.

◆   ◆   ◆

No man wants war if he is to fight it personally to kill or be killed. No sane man. The BAR man who would not fire his weapon when he was beside me in the ditch, was not unique. Thousands of soldiers during the Civil War loaded their rifle muzzles with multiple balls and never fired a shot. They went through the motions of loading, aiming and then loading again without firing their rifles. In Gettysburg, after the battle, thousands of rifles were found to have multiple loads and unfired.

In World War II, 75 to 80 percent of the soldiers never fired their rifles. This was approximately the same of all the previous wars. Men are not that eager to shoot the enemy as they are of saving their skin.

The biggest act of courage for a person who fights on the front lines is to leave his hole, his trench, his rock, or hiding place, and expose himself to the enemy as he moves foreword, or retreats, in fear. It takes a combination of bravery and fear to force yourself to leave a secure position and expose yourself to death. And you are commanded to do that over and over.

Sometimes Generals will visit the front lines and they are fearless. Fear is contagious so they won't display it if they had it anyway. Many through history have made their brief appearance before their front line troops to boost morale. They chose a quiet time and are accompanied with smart looking staff officers, and at times by reporters and photographers who record the event. They try to give the troops the illusion that there is no danger. They always smile and joke, like one of the troops which they are not. After a few minutes they are back where they belong in safe areas looking at maps, and the troops remain where they belong, up front.

Washington did this, Lee, Grant, Napoleon, the Caesars, all the Generals of all the wars. Their visits are so important that they are memorialized in emotional paintings hung in museums and government halls to prove that they too participated in the agony.

The Commanding General on our island was killed during the last days of the fighting. He was close to the front lines when a mortar burst near him and hit a coral formation, blowing a chunk of coral off which spun in the wind at an angle determined by fate and hit him in the chest. Not a mortar fragment, but a piece of coral killed him. That's how death came. Quick, at times improbable, and always final, of course. Appropriate medals were awarded for him. They even invent medals for generals if they don't have one.

I won't write the General's name here. It has been printed every time the battle is written about, because a General is an important person. I will only give him the same space as the rest of the men killed who are not mentioned in the records by name, but only numbers. Perhaps he was casualty 15,501 or 15,502. Just another number. In the end, it is all about numbers. Numbers killed, numbers wounded. Dollars spent.

Depending on who you read or listen to, the General's ability was either good or bad. Many say he should have done this and others say he should have done that. But after he died I think all arguments were superfluous. Had he lived he was to be acknowledged as, "The Conqueror Of Okinawa," according to one of his obituaries.

Then who were the dead boys in those jeeps?

◆   ◆   ◆

Most every day on the northern part of the island we were on patrol. As you patrol, especially at the point, your senses are alive with expectation. You are aware of your immediate world more than ever before for the simple reason that as you walk your life may be snuffed out immediately. Your eyes are sharp and searching. Perhaps a spider web has been disturbed in your path or is intact and tells you there has been movement in the area or not. Foot prints, broken branches, a discarded piece of paper or cloth, all carry important information.

Your ears are open to every sound that you can concentrate in them and transform into intelligence. Whispers, a snap of a twig, bird songs, insect calls, a foreign word or friendly, all alert the ears.

The nose is sensitive to that new odor. The smell of Japanese. They had a particular smell about them as people do and you found it in their camps, caves and hide outs. You caught it lingering in the air briefly and then intensely as you got closer. It was a stuffy, musky smell, of something constantly damp and wet. It was a strong mixture of old, dried fish, cooked rice and acrid smoke of burning reeds, charcoal or bamboo.

Every time you came across one of their camps that had been surprised and overrun there would be rice and tea boiling, and dried fish flakes open in little packets of thin paper. Frequently there were men with their toes on the trigger of their rifles, the rifle muzzles in his mouth and their heads blown open. They had tired of the war. The same smell was there.

Your eyes look for bobby traps, for a hidden sniper, for something that could kill you. You are wary of the living and of the dead who could be feigning or be bobby trapped to explode when you touched them. Even children at play suddenly startle you and you swing your rifle towards them with your finger on the trigger ready to squeeze.

Your finger is on the trigger and the safety is off and all you have to do is apply pressure; death and pain will occur where you hit. Each turn in the path, each push through a shrub, each walk through an open field, means life or death. Your senses cannot relax. They are exhausted at the end of the patrol for being alert so long. It is as though you have peeled off your skin to increase the sensitivity of your nerves to the slightest danger.

◆   ◆   ◆

The nights on the island often found trapped civilians trying to escape danger. There were several hundred thousand civilians living here and they looked very much like the enemy to us and were treated as such. We would kill over one hundred thousand of these people in three months including women and many young children..

We were warned that the civilians often were actually enemy soldiers in disguise, or were sympathizers and aided the enemy by killing Americans. This was a problem when you were on guard duty at night and you heard the movement of civilians. Were they friendly and harmlessly trying to get out of the way, or were they sheltering the enemy among them who would emerge and shoot at any moment?

I was doing guard duty with Karnes one clear moonlit night and we could see the stars continuing their journey into eternity as we sat in our foxhole position on a small hill. We were constantly on alert for noises of approaching enemy and at times our imaginations overcame our senses and made them see and hear things that were not there. Sometimes I wondered if Lee was seeing things clearly as he squinted through his thick glasses.

We were not at a front line and had chosen this high position to dig in for the night. In the morning we would resume patrolling. The bright moon illuminated the hill below us so if anyone approached we had a easy target. I risked lighting a cigarette under my poncho to hide the glare. We passed the butt back and forth in our cupped hands to conceal the glow.

In the still of the night we heard a voice, a whisper, a rustle of people walking. Children stifling a sob, a groan, a muffled curse. They were too noisy for soldiers. "Civilians," we whispered to each other.

We knew soldiers are trained not to move so noisily in the night.

The bright moon gave them away as they approached up a narrow path that led from the bottom of the hill, and we could see them very clearly. Lee had his BAR, and I, my rifle. They were about seventy five yards away from us down the hill and moving slowing across our position. In similar situations men on guard duty could immediately opened fire on the group. They were forgiven for killing civilians at night without question. Better dead civilians than dead Marines, was the accepted rational.

Lee realized that among them there could be an enemy soldier trying to get into our lines. But this was not really too plausible. Most of the times the enemy in this area was not moving at night mixing with civilians, especially groups that included children. This was a small group carrying bundles of household supplies on their heads. We could see them clearly. We identified woman and children.

There was no one to give us orders. Should we fire on the civilians? We had guard duty for two hours and we were on our own while the men slept behind us. It was our choice to determine if enemy soldiers were among the civilians or if the civilians were friendly.

Lee was in charge because he had the automatic weapon and could spray the group with heavy fire. If he fired on them the entire company in foxholes behind us would be up and ready to fire too. If he let them pass across the line they could be killed when they contacted other Marine units. He did not want to fire and kill women and children and innocent men, but he wanted to warn them that we were there on the hilltop waiting and watching, so they would chose another route.

Lee took the cigarette from my cupped hand and left it open to the night and took several long drags on the cigarette to expose the glow to the civilians below.

The cigarette glow sent a ripple of excitement into the group and there was a rustle of sounds and whispers and a soft scurrying as they disappeared into the opposite direction and into the brush. The rest of the night was quiet.

◆   ◆   ◆

Karnes and I would talk about many subjects including religion. This was an important subject to him and me because we both had so many doubts. He felt guilty for having doubts and at the same time he relied on his religion to save his life.

I, however, did not feel guilty about my doubts. I was ignorant about my religion compared to Lee. I doubted everything, but in times of danger I would silently repeat the Hail Mary prayer over and over like a frightened hypocrite. I was a hypocrite, I know, but relied on God to forgive me that, and for being human. I rationalized that since God made man, and me, if there were any imperfections they were His fault.

We talked about death, or "buying the farm" or "getting it."

Lee told me about the truest act of kindness that can never be repaid is honoring the dead. He said his father was a Chevra Kadisha volunteer. They volunteer to ensure that Jews are properly prepared and attended for burial when they die.

"The tradition goes back more than 2000 years," Lee said.

"That's even before Christ", I calculated. "You're kidding me?"

He said, "No, it is true," and then told me that Jesus was a Jew. My mouth dropped open on this news and automatically I took offense. Then Lee told me the facts which sounded plausible.

I said, "The nuns had never told me Christ was a Jew. I thought he was an Italian." Lee laughed.

Lee explained that the primary function of a Chevra Kadisha was to maintain a constant vigil over the dead body so the soul is comforted before it ascends into heaven, to wash and dress the body, and to ask forgiveness. He told me a lot of details about the way a person is dressed and the prayers that were said, but I forgot them.

"No one here will do this for me if I die," Lee said.

I promised I would at least perform the first requirement, the Shimira, he called it, if I survived. I would never leave his body until the graves registration people came, and I hoped it was enough time for his soul to leave his body. I had promised Krup to write to his mother and father should he "get it". We all wondered if we would "get it", how we would "get it", when we would "get it". We were all making covenants with each other if we got it, and with God, not to "get it".

◆   ◆   ◆

It was a sunny afternoon in May of 1944 and our squad of Marines came upon a clearing out of the woods very cautiously. Trained to expect death around any corner we distrusted the smell of smoke and moved cautiously.

A fire was burning in the dry dirt that blew about like talcum powder as our boots disturbed it. A young girl was on the ground twisting and turning her naked body in agitated movements. She looked like she was having a epileptic seizure. The young Marines looked on in amusement and some in disgust. Who was this fat, young girl alone in this farm clearing? She was a teenager, or not much older. Her skin was very white, almost albino and her hair black, all covered by the powdery dust.

The men circled the girl and looked about the clearing into the nearby trees to see if anyone was about.

A trap? A weird joke? What?

"What the hell is she doing here?"

"Don't ask me, No one else is around this fucking place."

"Maybe she is part of a trap. The Japs put her here for some reason."

"Shoot her." Several others nodded.

"Yeah, let's shoot her."

Several weeks of easy war, mainly of patrolling and killing pockets of snipers, still had brutalized us enough to think like that.

"You shoot her and you'll have to shoot me," I said.

"The Poet is a crazy son of bitch," one said. "He'll do it too."

Krup was embarrassed by my theatrics.

"Take it easy, Lance, they are just talking. They won't hurt her."

I knew that Krup would not allow it either.

Perhaps if the girl were pretty and attractive the men would have raped her as very many were raped during the campaign. No one considered that. She was twisting in the dirt and drooling, her eyes rolled back in their sockets. She had no pubic hair, and her body was spotted with insect bites and a rash that made her repulsive, and discouraged sexual fantasies.

"Well, what the hell are we going to do with her?"

"We're ordered to stay here until relieved."

"We may be here all night and she'll make noise and attract attention."

"What a frigging mess."

There were no Corpsman around to give the girl first aid of any kind and we did not know what to do. We were reluctant to touch her. After a while she became quiet and lay in the dirt silently and did not move. We scouted about the small farm to see what we could find of interest.

It was getting to mid day and we had not eaten for some time. We searched for possible food.

A rooster walked near us, pecking on the ground, and one of the Marines pulled out his forty five and shot at it. He hit it in the upper leg and the chicken ran hopping about with its severed the leg gushing blood but still hanging on the body by bit of skin. We all ran after the bird to kill it but it eluded us by frantically hopping about on its one leg. Finally a Marine caught it and twisted its neck. He was splattered with blood. We laughed at the dark comedy of chasing a one legged bird, and the bloody Marine.

I wanted to kill something for myself. I wanted to kill something just to shoot my weapon. A skinny, old farm horse was grazing nearby and I decided that I would kill it. I was carrying a carbine instead of my regular rifle and don't remember why. I had never fired it. I approached the horse as it lowered its head to nibble on some grass and placed the muzzle a few inches from its head just above the eyes. The horse was brown and spotted with patches of white. Its ribs were visibly outlined against it its skin.

I imagined where the brain was so that I could hit it and the horse would die quickly, cleanly without pain. I pulled the trigger hoping that it would misfire and prevent what I was about to do. If had misfired I know I would not have tried again.

The horse gave a pained cry and lifted its head high in the air before letting it fall to the ground with a slap. Trembling and jerking in spasms of pain and ensuing death, its mouth opened showing old, yellow teeth streaked with blood. Its large, brown-gray eyes looked at me like two bulging mirrors conveying nothing, only reflecting the light of the day. They did not show surprise, fear, terror or any animal questioning, but I read an accusation in them.

I became frightened when the horse did not die instantly and was bleeding from head and mouth into a red paste of blood it made in the dusty dirt. Its body twitched and jerked. Its muscles gave small trembles, and the nerves along its flanks flickered in a series of small throbs.

Die, die, please die. I wanted to end the experience, but the horse continued to live.

I then quickly shot it in the head several more times quickly to stop the quivering and our mutual pain.

Even after the additional shots, the body lived.

The large chest heaved gently, stubbornly holding to life.

No one questioned me. We were all killing animals to eat and for sport.

It was just an old horse, I, the Poet, explained to myself and anyone who questioned, but that did not mitigate my guilt.

I had joined the killers.

The death of the horse was of no importance to anyone but the farmer who would suffer the pain of losing his animal because of my adolescent experimentation. Why did I vacillate so quickly from champion to monster? First I wanted to protect the naked girl and then, moments later, I killed the horse. I could never explain this acceptably to myself with all the words I hunted to write the truth.

Several Marines were cleaning the amputated rooster the best they could with a little water we contributed from our canteens and heated over a small fire.

Dusk had slipped in before we could do a good job of cleaning the bloody bird and we were full of the sticky chicken blood as we pulled the guts and feathers from the body. It had to be cooked before dark. We had a small fire going which we tried to hide with our ponchos and backs to but we could not prevent smoke from rising.

A farm boy Marine stuck the bird on to a piece of tree branch and made a makeshift roasting spit. He stuck the severed leg into the cavity along with some grass to hold it in place. Soon the entire area was permeated with the smell of burning chicken fat and chicken feathers. We knew that soon the fire had to be extinguished as the darkness came or it would put us in danger. Although we were not in the front lines, the enemy was not far away.

In spite of the cover we had given the small fire it glowed more brightly as the day darkened and it was soon noticed by one of the other Marine units. A voice called out, "Put out that fire before we all get shot, you damn shit heads."

Grumbling, we kicked dirt into the small fire pit after removing the chicken which was burnt and still mostly raw. We tore pieces of the carcass from the bird and passed them around to eager hands. The blood and juices of the bird dripped from our lips and down our chins but there were words of approval all around. You could hear the teeth grinding the uncooked muscle and sinew and when we swallowed the meat there were soft sighs for the taste of flesh.

As we ate the chicken in the dark, the naked girl somehow had disappeared into the darkness and underbrush. We never saw her again.

The flies and maggots would soon begin their role in consuming the body of the dead horse that lay in the dust close by, but I could not look at it. I could feel its disturbing presence in the night, as at times, I still do now.

◆   ◆   ◆

Many children lost their families during the fighting and bombing. They were not always taken into the caves by Japanese or civilians. The young, naked girl in the dirt who had disappeared could have been one of them. It was a time of terror for the civilians including children. Many children had to survive on their own for days before being sent to a safe area. Some would be raped, or killed by the Japanese, but most would be killed by Americans, or their own people in mass suicides.

Many times when we entered the small, thatched cottages looking for enemy we would find a person who had his or her head sliced off by a sword. It was a Japanese type of execution. Perhaps it was an act of revenge or a robbery. Someone may have taken advantage of the confusion of war to settle a score or to steal something.

We slept that night on the ground we stood on eating our chicken dinner not far from the dead horse.. The smell of chicken and chicken blood remained with us through the night because we did not want to waste water for washing.

As the new morning began, the mist was still heavy on the fields and the sun had difficulty burning through the haze. The air was filled with a mouth watering smell of frying bacon.

A Marine had slaughtered the farmer's fat sow and hung in up by its hamstrings the night before in preparation for the next day's meal. Again, one of the farm boy Marines from the South had expertly slit the pig's belly open and allowed five or six piglets embryos fall into a pit he had dug below the hanging animal. The animal's meat was pink and anemic looking because of its pregnancy, but over the fire that morning it smelled like prime bacon cooking as an occasional gust of wind blew the smoke our way.

We were cleaning our equipment and eating partially cooked pig meat when we were alerted by the sound of aircraft engines that roared as they flew between the valleys of the mountains. In the distance we could see the outlines of two aircraft which came out of the mountains shooting at each other as they flew low over the valley and hop scotched over the smaller hills. The roar of the motors and the burst of gun fire from their machine guns made it all seem like a movie being filmed for our entertainment. When they flew closer over our heads we could see that the red ball on the wing of the plane that was the aggressor.

"The meat ball," we called it, the symbol of the rising sun.

"The fucking meatball is after that Corsair. He must be in trouble and trying to get away. He doesn't seem to be shooting back."

We loved to see our planes win in any fight, and when they were unleashing their rockets into mountain caves we cheered when the plane kept diving closer and closer to the cave's entrance so that the impact and accuracy of the rockets would be greater. When a pilot prolonged his dive until the last minute to fire rockets into the cave we would shout with pride, "he must be a Marine pilot."

Both Marine and Navy pilots flew the Corsair fighter which had upswept wings that could be folded when not in flight, and were easy to identified.

If a pilot just took a short dive towards the cave, released his rockets and flew quickly away we, laughed, "he must be a Navy pilot."

The two planes above us continued their dog fight and then suddenly disappeared behind a large hill where there was an explosion followed by a curl of black smoke which climbed into the sky.

We were ordered to examine what happened and began running double time towards the black smoke. As we got closer we could hear the sputter of the fire and smell the burning of material and aviation fuel. Then we could see the aircraft and the swept wing that had been thrown away from the impact site. We who knew the Corsair wing understood what had happened before we saw the fuselage burning. The fire was now mostly gone and only the material scorched by the extreme heat continued to smolder. No human form was visible at or near the cockpit. Another wing of the Corsair had broken free and we could see the American star underneath.

A black mass that looked like a ball of tar lay between the fuselage and the second wing. Approaching closer we could see that the black ball was the body of the pilot who still had his parachute pack strapped to him and was smoldering. It looked like the pilot had drawn himself up into a fetal position as he burned and was almost completely consumed by the fire.

Somehow the parachute material itself had survived the flames and we were able to unravel it from its pack to wrap the pilot in it. My brain kept flicking me back to the Worcester plane crash that I guarded with Chief and to the burnt pilot in front of us. The stark whiteness of the parachute was accentuated when we wrapped what remained of the burnt, black body of the pilot in it. There was enough material to wrap him several times.

There was no way to identify the man and we left him near the plane knowing that personnel would soon be sent to locate and identify him. We did not worry about those details, and only sadly wished that he had won the fight. How the Japanese pilot claimed his victory, I don't know, but I do know that his victory did nothing to save his country.

For a long time I associated the memory of the burnt dead pilot with the smell of pork we had eaten that morning.

◆　　　　◆　　　　◆

We continued our patrolling. Because the island was honeycombed with caves of all sizes, we patrolled from cave to cave killing whoever was inside. At times there were enemy and at other times civilian. Many times there were both enemy and civilians sharing a cave, and some caves were enormous. If the cave was small the ordinary Private could throw a hand grenade into it and consider it secured. Larger caves required flamethrowers or satchel charge experts to burn and blow them up or seal the openings. It was a mundane operation, moving forward someone would spot a cave and we would surround it and approach cautiously until we could blow it up or burn it out.

If the cave was occupied, the survivors inside had no choice but to run out into the clear air when the fire and smoke found them. Or they died.

They came out coughing and crying, men, women, and children. Their eyes burning and their cloths smoldering with burning phosphorus that could not be extinguished and ate through clothing into the flesh and into the bone. The pain was horrible to witness especially when children were the victims.

Two Marines were laughing, insanely excited by the brutality and their own fear. They laughed at a mother clutching her baby and trying to wipe the phosphorous off the baby's clothing. They had been calloused to the point of inhumanity. Were these my countrymen? Was I any better?

The chance that this cave had Japanese soldiers in it was remote. The island was full of small caves where the civilians sought shelter from the war. They just wanted to get out of the way and survive. The Japanese threw many of them out into the open from the larger caves that they fortified and the civilians had to find small caves for their families.

"You, dumb sons of bitches," I shouted at the two Marines. "Look what you've done. They are only women and kids. Civilians."

They knew my reputation that could dramatically erupt at the sight of injustice did not argue when I began to shout obscenities which I knew quite well. They knew too that I was able to become dangerous and unreasonable if provoked enough. They were not going to take chances as I swung my rifle towards them.

"One more grenade and I'll blow your heads off," I warned. The suffering of the civilians had overwhelmed me.

They stopped laughing. And I knew they would not do any more harm. There was no reason to. I tried to help the civilians who were now shouting and crying and rolling in the dirt in their fear and pain.

"Corpsman," I shouted.

Sometimes this helped if you got the right Corpsman to hear you..

"Are you becoming a gook lover, Poet?," one of the bastards shouted at me as I picked phosphorus from a women's clothing with my K-Bar knife.

In my heart I was ready to cut them down more easily than fighting the enemy or shooting a horse. But this was war. This was the game played whether I liked it or not. They were on my side and these people were gooks to them, but not to me. I never considered them as gooks only people who been caught in the terrible injustice of war. I detested, and highly resented being a part of this insanity that would cause such suffering. I had not volunteered for this!

A half naked boy of about nine or ten years holding his left wrist with his right hand came walking down the path near us. He had a clean bullet hole in his left shoulder. By clean I mean it was not bleeding and the hole the bullet made left a little, round hole. I pulled out my sulfa bandage pack we carried on our cartridge belts and placed the bandage against the boy's wound. Remarkably it was not bleeding but I wanted to keep it clean and protect the hole.

The boy said nothing. He did not whimper or thank me or smile. He just held his left wrist with his right hand and kept walking along the path. Perhaps he was in shock. I don't know. I felt good that I had helped him a little. Then as he walked pass me I saw that he had a hole in the back of his shoulder where the bullet had exited. I had no more bandages and called for a medical Corpsman again without luck and the little boy kept walking toward nowhere.

More people were now coming out of the cave, men women, and children. They walked out into the daylight blinking, and shivering with fear. Some were wounded severely and some slightly, and they all had that puzzled and cowering demeanor of people turned into animals by fear. They had been told by the Japanese the Americans would kill them and that was true in some cases. So they were apprehensive. They did not know what to expect from the enemy who had been bombing their little island for so long and driving them to live in caves and the tombs of their ancestors.

The casualties from the cave continued to come out. Many died as they did and lay with the wounded in the dirt. A civilian man who was bleeding from a stomach wound was moaning in terrible pain as Marines milled around him. One called for a Corpsman who was busy and was not rushing to get to the civilian. There was little that he could do in any case. The wounded man pointed to the Marine rifles and then to his head getting his point across quite clearly.

Smoke, stench, confusion, and fear filled the air as it always does after a massacre and there was little time for evaluation and argument.

A great and obscene courage was requested by this dying man and it would not result in the award of a medal designed by governments. It would not be awarded the ubiquitous medal acknowledging the loss of blood. Everyone including me chose to disregard the request except LaFoo who took his .45 that he had requisitioned from a dead officer and calmly placed it to the suffering man's head as the man looked up at him thankfully.

The look in LaFoo's eyes as he pulled the trigger, and soon after as his soul was ripped away, cannot be described. The society of men have never developed dictionaries containing those words. They are not words used to describe football games. So I offer, his soul was ripped away.

LaFoo turned and smiled at us. It was a smile closer to a scream without sound. He said nothing and no one dared say anything to him. It was all said in the action. Bravery, fear, savage brutality and compassion. What exactly LaFoo felt in his heart no one will ever know. But I remembered the story he had told us about tracking the wounded deer through the woods in New Hampshire until he could mercifully kill it. But this was not the same.

Ever since that day he never tried to save himself from the shells that exploded near him. As we crouched and sought shelter in a hole from an incoming round, LaFoo would just continue a conversation as though nothing happened. He did not question our defensive behavior and fright. He did not smile or laugh or show bravado in any way. I believe he was a man who had partnered with death.

◆   ◆   ◆

For centuries the citizens of this island buried their ancestors in oval shaped tombs built above ground against a sloping rise. A small, movable slab located in the front of the tomb afforded easy entry. Many of us used the tombs as brief shelters during the rains that flooded us in our foxholes, and the civilians used them, too, for the same purpose. An average size man could stand in a crouched position inside and the tomb could hold several people, and they were remarkable dry.

The occupants of the tombs were in various forms of desiccated decomposition but there was no unpleasant odor, just a soft mustiness. The occupants had shriveled, dried, and mummified but their hair and nails continued to grow. Those who had been in the tombs for a long time had been reduced to dust and bones, and some of the Marines took the skulls as souvenirs carrying them in their packs for a while as a joke. But this was not during combat. During combat we saw many corpses of our own and did not want to be carrying a skull around to play games with.

The Okinawans were never accepted as equals by the Japanese despite sharing a similar culture. The war had in a few weeks destroyed most the world they knew. They were innocents in a terrible process that would kill more than one hundred thousand of them before it was over. Many of their women would be raped and many families would commit suicide together rather than trust the fickle humanity of Americans or Japanese.

I learned the futility of their position when I bandaged the little boy who was shot in the shoulder. I had one bandage issued by the Marine Corps and it was to be used on myself if I were shot. That bandage I had applied on the wounded boy was all I had to bandage the world, and it was not even enough to finish the job of bandaging the second hole in his back.

5

Butcher Shop

Nations plan long and hard to ensure that they get full value from their soldiers. They know they will be exposed to war, one of the most horrifying and traumatic acts a human being can participate in. Combat will psychologically wound 98 percent of all who participate in it for a length of time. And the two percent who are not driven insane by war probably were insane already. John Gabriel, *No More Heroes,*

There are few things as terrifying as an eighteen year old boy dressed in a fatigue uniform, a steel helmet on his head, two slings of ammunition across his chest, two hand grenades hooked to the ammunition belt around his waist, and a rifle in his hands, walking towards you slowly and deliberately. You fear all the armament and ammunition he carries, but there is something else that should make you extremely anxious as he approaches. The few sprigs of hair growing on his face is the face of youth, and he has been told by some authority to destroy you and by god, he will, unless he is killed or overcome with fear.

I know, because I was one of them, and I could see the fear in the faces of men, woman and children when I and other Marines approached in small farms and villages of places we had never heard about a few days before. There is an excitement in being feared. It transforms humans into little gods who strut about believing that it is all important and real, and that they are really indestructible and immortal. It is such a exciting (and false) feeling of immortality, and power that only the very young can feel it. Our young minds transformed each of us into play actors occupying narcissistic center stage until the insane terror pushed us off.

Barely out of childhood, we were weaned on Hollywood propaganda, and were anxious to explore the world with all the emotions and joys that excited a young body. The body, so supple and pliable, so full of newly emerging cells that were still developing into what they we're programmed to become, received a message from the brain that it was invincible, and the body believed it was true.

Feeling immortal made us dangerous until the brain became frightened enough and learned otherwise.

The young body could walk for hours and days with little food and rest. It could sleep in holes half filled with water; it could sleep without the supple joints stiffening and aching in the morning. The few older men with us who were in their late twenties, or early thirties already knew what arthritis was. We called them, Pop, or Old Man. But we could not understand and would not for many years, if we lived.

Everything the senses saw, tasted and felt and smelled was accepted by our young bodies with the full initial impact of first awareness. Never again would the senses be so alive and invincible, dangerous, and vulnerable.

At that age the brain has not completely absorbed the teachings of humanity. At that age almost anything unpredictable and brutal can happened, and usually does.

The United States wanted those young bodies when the country got into war. It got Hollywood to glamorize the war for the youth who would fight it, identified a demon enemy to hate, and told all the young men that they were invincible warriors and heroes.

Then the government took those bodies and tried to prove it was right.

◆   ◆   ◆

We were slowly climbing the cave burrowed hills rolling before us. The spit of automatic fire was intermittent but persistent and never hesitated for more than a few seconds before continuing. A stuttered spitting, pit, pit, pit, spit tit tit titting of bullets. Some by aim, but most by chance, hit targets of flesh and bone which were entered and broken. You could hear the scream from the targets that were hit. You could see the red from the flesh gush out the skin. You could hear the cursing and screams of pain. Shouts of fear and hatred mingled with cries of agony.

We had not seen so many dead and dying men in our young lives. We were all just bags of skin assuming names and other attributes of humans, but essentially just bags of skin encompassing flesh, bones, organs, blood, and tissue. The bag of skin was holding us together, and trying to protect all it contained.

If something broke into the bag of skin it began to bleed. If left on the field in the open the dead bag of skin would begin to rot and expand with internal gases that fester and fill the skin with a foul, putrefied stench. The bag of skin turns black and purple, yellow and green, fills with pus and it bursts under the internal pressure of putrid gas.

It is not a person anymore just a bag of skin. You want to get it quickly out of your sight and bury it. If it is one of our bags of skin or one of theirs, the sight is about the same.

You want to hide from it and its ghastly reminder of what could be you. Sometimes the bags of skin fill so much with maggots and gases that they begin to come apart where it wore a belt, or bulges against a buttoned jacket and bursts into a mass of eating maggots.

This is not a clean butcher shop, this is Hell on earth. The nightmare of battle. We continue walking up the hill killing and burning, and the enemy shoot at us from their caves until they are killed or wounded. Many die. Many are ripped apart and continue to live. The bag of skin, torn and shattered, continues to hold the vital parts together and bleeds for a while. It is only wounded now.

We continue this insanity all day and then steal a moment to eat next to a bag of skin that is beginning to rot in the sunlight. It doesn't take long for the maggots to begin feasting in the open wound. We swipe away the fat, obscenely colored flies that feast on the corpses and then try to share our food, too. They are not easily discouraged. At times we swallow flies with our meals. We look at the bag of skin smothered with flies and maggots and continue forward urged by shouts of men who think they are in charge of this chaotic insanity. Men with authority.

Most bullets miss. They fly into space and land harmlessly between blades of grass or next to a flower or a clump of clover. Some lodged into the dirt deeply and split small stones and are buried forever or until someone finds them while planting rice or a cabbage patch. Some lodged into trees and the trees healed over the bullets and they became part of the tree forever. Most bullets just expend themselves uselessly after missing targets and tumble to harmless immobility.

The large artillery shells make a thudding sound when they hit. These could be mortars, or shells from guns rolled out from the cave in the distant mountain. They are rolled out to the mouth of the cave, fired and then rolled back in by an enemy who has zeroed in the killing range very accurately.

When the bullets found their target they zipped through flesh and bone spilling the red over the grass and dirt. These big bombs sometimes exploded and sent out pieces of themselves. These were called fragments. As the fragments swished into the air they made unique sounds depending on their sized and shape. Whosssshh, was one sound they made, flipppop op op op, was another sound the big bullets and raw metal made. Zuh suh suh zuh uh uh uh and eeeing eeeezing zeeinng could be a tiny one, sharp as a razor and when it hit the target it zig zagged through tissue and organs and sliced fine pieces that the clever surgeons would never find to repair.

Sometimes these slivered pieces of shells cut quickly into livers, hearts, kidneys, bladders and testicles. Sometimes the target died quickly and sometimes not. But the target usually had a chance of freeing at least one sound from his mouth even if it was only a sound of surprise like, "wahh?", and then the target was dead.

Sometimes the target cried for hours after being hit.

We kept climbing, burning, and shooting, crazed to terror as the nightmare played about us. We moved slowly because it was dangerous and we were afraid to move into danger. Men around us died but we could not see anyone shooting at us. Death came from anonymous killers.

Then the flame throwers burned and hissed into the holes where the enemy was hiding and praying to be back in Tokyo with their families eating dinner. What did they eat? Fish heads and rice. We all knew that joke; the gooks ate fish heads and rice. The gooks, hah!

The fat, red tongue of the flame thrower licked out with a lazy hiss, curled black at its tip, and then retreats. If the flame touched someone he would turn black and burst into fire. The flame sucked the air out of his lungs before it could rise to his throat and his brain instruct his tongue to form a scream. Soon the man would be a twisted, blackened rag doll grotesquely twisted as his body shriveled from the fire. If he ran out into the open we were ready to shoot bullets through his burning body. He would end up on the ground burnt and distorted like some over done animal, a sheep or a goat or a dog. Sometimes he would retain the human shape and you knew it had been a man. All roasted men look alike when there is no uniform.

The burnt flesh gave out a remarkably sweet odor. Some said chicken. Well done. I never thought of humans as an animal product. Now I did.

The dead looked like soft, twisted manikins, rag dolls, corpses; some burnt, some missing parts of their bodies, some drained of blood quickly and some bright red with blood trickling out of their wounds.

They were broken bags of skin and not to be feared anymore. Just rag dolls dead in the dirt and smashed under the treads of a tank until the head was three times its original size. Sometimes the tanks went over the head and body until it was a gingerbread man. A rag doll gingerbread man. It was grotesquely comical to see a rag doll with a head about three times the usual size and as flat as a dusty pancake. Real funny. Sometimes the fragment would cut the top of a doll's skull and expose the soft, gray jelly of his brain. It shimmered like a cup of raw oysters above two eyes that gazed out at the world in puzzlement.

We continued walking up the slope towards the high point overlooking a city called Naha. The main city of this butcher shop island.

A piece of bone here, a bit of flesh there. I tried guessing what part of the body these fragments came from. Was it part of a leg, arm, ribs, hip? You could tell the head easily if still in tact, but little was. Look! I think that's a jaw bone. You can see some teeth still in place. Here's a foot, a hand, some guts, a leg, a torso. What's that? Can't tell.

A sane butcher shop was orderly, But these butchers were untidy and mad. At the animal butcher the parts are displayed in cases and you knew where they came from. They are labeled for you to read what was in the packages. There were labels that identified the liver, kidney, heart, tripe and soup bones, and all the other bits and pieces of a dead animal.

There was no order here. No packaging. Everything was crude and dirty. No clean cut separated the ribs from the torso. Tenderloin and chuck were ripped apart indiscriminately clinging to each other without reason. We were ripping each other apart by mad butchery using twisted steel and explosives and devouring each other alive.

The professional butcher knew his cuts of meat and where they belonged. No one here knew exactly what piece belonged to which bag of skin of either side when they were torn and burned in that blasphemous way.

To the right, as we climbed over the gore and kicked rocks and dirt on those behind us the sun was beginning its daily dip into the horizon. Darkness would soon be spreading over the larger islands of Japan just three hundred and fifty miles away, and the charcoal fires of millions of homes would begin to glow as the evening meal was prepared. In Kyushu a mother prayed to Buddha for her son while in Brooklyn another prayed to Jesus for hers. They prayed, all the mothers, in Japanese and in Polish, in English and Spanish, all the languages that could form the word God in this world.

We finally reached the top of the hills where we could see the city of Naha below burning, and shattered. A few skeletons of buildings hung precariously above the ground. They were silhouetted black against setting sun, insisting on standing although their interiors had been smashed and blown away. The rest was in shambles. Under the debris of the city were thousands of bags of skin beginning to expand and putrefy. Many were little babies.

We dug foxholes to form a line from the high cliff on our right that ran down into the waters of the sea far below. To the far left our Army units that had climb similar hills, formed a front line against the enemy for the night. Behind us were replacements units and pockets of overrun enemy still hidden in caves. When it got dark they would be coming out to find lost units and to kill us.

Night crept in on little cat feet. Carl Sandburg's poem, *Fog*, I thought, "The fog comes on little cat feet, It sits looking over the harbor and city...". My mind searched for the words. Naha and its harbor smoldered below.

Because our energy was spent and our hunger keen, the foxholes for the night were shallow. It had been a long day that still had time to run with surprises for all. Later when gunfire would start again we would try to dig deeper into the earth and pile the loose dirt and stones around the foxholes to protect ourselves but then it would be too late.

Orders were to remain in your foxhole or risk being shot. The pass word for the night was, 'lollypop', hard for Japanese tongue to roll over the tongue, rendering it 'rorrypop', we hoped. I never heard the enemy try to use one of our passwords except in the movies.

As the darkness saturated us more deeply the Japanese soldiers came out of their overrun caves and tried to return to their units. In doing so they had to cross the line we had set up for the night.

In the confusion of the dark night men shouted and cursed at each other. English and Japanese words whispered in the night. The gunfire from various directions and the running of frightened men joined in turmoil and confused fear. Nothing could be seen clearly until a flare illuminated when it burst overhead. It made a popping sound and then burst into a few seconds of bright, sputtering light that descended slowly by parachute. And then it returned to a deeper blackness as the retina fought to adjust.

As the night progressed, confusion and fear became partners to exacerbate our world of gunfire, urine and rotting human flesh. The latter so oppressive and intense that you absorbed it through your skin by osmosis. You tasted in your mouth, over your tongue, after smelling with your nose.

Scenes of tragic comedy occurred as we accidentally encounter each other in the night and screamed in fear. They run over our foxholes stepping on the helmeted men and fell to the ground wrestling with themselves and at times with us. They stumbled into holes occupied by men who want to kill them and escaped clumsily in terror. They hid against a wall or tree shivering in fear, forgetting all the training games and lectures and are shot where they cower. The fear too, seemed tangible and contagious, an ever-changing virus that permeated the rocky hills and infected both sides with equal virulence. You witness its symptoms in the scurry of the Japanese as they tried to make it across the line to reach their own troops.

You could sense it too in the hushed voices of the Japanese and the Americans as they tried to communicate with their own men not knowing who was which. Only the wounded disobeyed the caution to be silent. Their screams and moans continued in the darkness through the night and their pleas for help and mercy never ended.

"Corpsman, Corpsman," that blood chilling call that told you someone was hurt and possibly dying, froze your heart.

"Mamma, God, Jesus, oh, mother," the wounded pleaded, screamed and swore into the night.

The Japanese wounded did the same. They called for mothers and sweethearts in their own language. They probably prayed to Buddha and their ancestors. They knew there was no medical help for them caught behind enemy lines and soon they were silent.

When a few moments of silence permitted the nerves to relax, we could hear the maddening hum of mosquitoes that came to suck our blood. We lay in the brief silence listening to the mosquito hum and then dive silently for blood. So much blood was flowing freely but still the mosquito had to puncture the skin to drink? The moon had hidden herself behind some clouds denying us her light to leave us in a deep black.

Between the foxholes men were moving and whispering in a hushed fear. Gunfire again, and then a grenade exploded close by. We tangled together trying to escape each other, and frighteningly killed or wounded each other and sometimes in that darkness, killed our own.

Is there a battle plan to all this? Will they write about it in detail and explain what happened here? How would this be recorded in history? Explain this madness on a lone hillside occupied by young men from alien countries all half mad with fear and all praying to be somewhere else?

I make no pretext to explain what all this meant to the failure or success of this battle. To explain it in historical terms only denigrates the emotions, passions and suffering of those who participated here. How can anyone logically explain madness? Historians will explain it all to us when it is over and tell us exactly how this small engagement fit into the broad fabric of the war, or more likely just forget it.

Another group of flares pop overhead and casts a false, and eerie light. In the brief moments of this light you try to distinguish reference points, foes and friends but it is all a confused, surreal, amateurish stage setting and everyone freezes under the brief light and then forgets what they have seen.

The light briefly exposed the insanity before the participants could hide from its glare. Those in nearby foxholes could be seen clearly as they crouched together for protection. The Japanese dropped where they stood when the flare came on, feigning death until the blackness returned. Feigning death did not always save them because both sides practiced shooting the dead for insurance.

Someone screamed that he was hit and then with a flurry of grunts they dragged the man to my hole where he took my place as I got out. I was out in the open but on my belly looking into the foxhole as a Corpsman began dressing the wound.

I tried digging another hole next to them but did not go deep digging on my belly. I dared not stand up. The man was hit in the chest and the Corpsman quickly ripped his jacket open and placed a bandage on the bleeding hole.

The bandage looked so white in the dark but soon it turned to the color of blood and then it turned black. The man called for Jesus, Mary and Joseph, and then his mother. He kept calling for his mother through the night. When a flare popped open in the sky I could see his face. He was from the Boston area. I remembered him. I didn't remember his name but remembered seeing him with his long Irish face. He was an older guy. I'd say he was at least twenty two. He could have been Collins, Murphy, Jones, Donnelly, any thousand of Irish names.

He was one of those Irish guys from Quincy, Weymouth, Concord, or Newtonville. He always spoke about going to Revere Beach and having fun with the girls. He liked to go to the Boston Common Canteen and talk to the girls who volunteered to cheer the boys. He liked to go to church with his family and his mother had taught him all about being a good Catholic.

He used to say, "Pak ma cah." instead of "Park my car."

"Hail Mary full of grace the lord is with thee, Holy Mary Mother of God, The fruit of thy womb Jesus, Jesus, Oh Jesus, Hail Mary full of grace the lord is with thee. Hail Mary full of grace the lord is with thee. Blessed art thee amongst all woman. Oh God, Oh God, Mom Oh Mom. Jesus, Mary and Joseph. Hail Mary mother of God the Lord is with thee. Blessed is…Oh mother, Jesus, God, Jesus, Hail Mary, mother of God Mary mother of God…the womb, the fruit of thy womb the womb, Jesus, Jesus, oh Jesus. Oh mother of God art thou amongst, Oh God Oh help me. Hail Mary mother of God. Hail Mary, Hail Mary, Hail Mary. Help meeeeee." I prayed silently, along with him, as he suffered through the night.

He called and prayed through most of the night and we whispered for him to be quiet.

"Shh, shh, shh," the Corpsman said as he gently adjusted the bandages and shot him full of morphine which not strong enough to stop the pain..

There were enemy around us. He did not hear nor care any longer. He kept praying and calling to his mother and we suffered his wound with him through the night

He prayed to the saints and his blood flowed from his terrible wound and his voice got weaker and then stopped. He had no blood left in him and he was dead. His face literally was white as snow, drained of all color that blood puts on our cheeks. I thought of the blood of Christ depicted on paintings at the Stations of the Cross in Saint Joseph's Church in Lodi, New Jersey. It was the same color. The same blood shed for the sins of man.

We lifted him out of the foxhole, covered him with a poncho, and I resumed my place there next to the another Marine. I eased myself back into the space I had loaned to the dead man, and a part of us died with him that night.

When things became quiet the mosquitoes continued sucking our blood. Voraciously feeding, they drove us mad with their constant buzzing followed by that silent moment when they landed and are ready to bite and drink.

I wet wads of toilet paper with my saliva and stuffed them in my ears to escape their buzzing, and placed my poncho over my head. A light drizzle hung in the humid air. In a few minutes the air under the poncho was stifling. I feared being killed while my ears were clogged with toilet paper and not being able to hear or see my killer approach. I risked it for a few moments to escape the mosquitoes, but soon removed the poncho and unplugged my ears letting the mosquitoes feed. The man next to me did the same.

Dead tired, we were falling asleep despite the danger, and the mosquitoes. We dared not risk sleeping long. We could not place guards because we were all intermingled with each other and the enemy. There was no clearly defined area of a front line here. If you shared a foxhole with someone, you could not trust each other to stay awake. You were both too tired.

You poked each other to keep awake. At moments the weariness overcame us and we nodded off into a wonderful unconsciousness only to recover almost immediately into startled awareness.

What was the password for the night? Lollypop? Or was that last night? Usually I forgot it before the night was over.

During the night, near dawn, someone whispered to me, "Kruplowski got it."

Whoever it was knew we were buddies and had risked crawling to my hole to tell me.

In the dark I said, "Oh, no!"

I was overcome with a raw feeling of sadness that was added to the anguish, discomfort, and fear of that night. It would become the one night in our lives we would remember until our last.

The drizzle hung over us like a shroud and the faint light of the new day slowly began to turn the horizon a light gray. All about the hill where we had dug foxholes were the wounded and the dead. The earth was stained with blood, shit and urine. Bandages with black blood and bits of flesh and bone marked where a Corpsman was at work a short while ago.

I couldn't believe Krup was dead until daylight came and I saw him on a stretcher.

His girlfriend, Wanda, in Quincy Massachusetts was waiting for him to come home and get married. She had his photos in uniform all over the house. His family in Conshohocken would get the terrible news soon. For a while I believed that I was acting in one of the Hollywood films again and that this was not real. Slowly, I began to accept the reality of it. This was not Hollywood anymore, not just pictures flickering on a screen.

I helped three other guys carry Krup down the hill in a stretcher. Each of us holding one of the stretcher handles walked down the hill over the butcher shop we had climbed the day before. He was a big guy and we had to rest several times on the way down. Once the stretcher was jostled and I got angry.

"Watch what the fuck you're doing," I warned the others, protecting my buddy.

We placed him among the others who were killed, all of them in a line. I made sure they didn't drop the stretcher or jostle it too much. I had pulled the poncho over Krup to hide his face. I wanted to protect his privacy. I did not want the world to see him dead.

I was ashamed that he had died. I wanted my buddy to be alive and strong. I wondered if his eyes were open but would not look to find out. I wondered where the wounds that killed him were, but I could not look.

His big, left arm stretched outside the poncho and I tried to place it along side his body but it would not move. It would not bend. I didn't know what rigor mortis was then, all I know he was stiff and his big, left arm stuck out of the poncho sadly. The large, silver Marine Corps ring with the globe, eagle and anchor was on one finger. He bought it the PX in Parris Island. All of us kids wore that cheap, silver ring at one time or other with pride.

I had thrown mine away a long time ago.

I had cried all the way down that rocky, butcher shop hill. I guarded Krup's body. We all knew that this dead body, and the others being laid in a row at the bottom of the hill had earned a special status now. In our so called, civilized society, they were heroes, not just bags of skin. Death had made them heroes.

I sat next to Krup to keep him company and protect him until they took him away, and I cried with deep despair and sadness in my teenage heart.

Then I did something that I had seen in a Hollywood movie. I began running about the hill shouting "I'll kill every frigging Jap I can see, I'll get the bastards who killed Krup and I ran from ditch to hole pretending that I was looking for Japs to kill. There was no one to kill. It was daylight and everything was safe for a while but I felt I had to play that scene I had seen in the movies.

Over the years recalling that time embarrassed me as it does now that I write about it. The Corps never told us how to react when a good friend was killed and you felt the pain in your guts. The only reference points I had for mourning were the movies that depicted a similar situation, so I played the roll as I had learned it from Hollywood.

We had levels of sadness as we have today in normal life. Someone's death is always sad, the man who died in my foxhole several hours before made me sad as I prayed with him through his agony, the many corpses around the hill made me sad, the Marines more than the Japanese, but the level of sadness had peaked in my heart when I lost Krup. His death would identify the high mark of sadness in my life. Others would match it. None would surpass it.

We kicked the Japanese soldiers over the side of the cliff to get them away from our sight, or covered them quickly with dirt and rocks where they lay. We buried only enough of their bodies to hide them from the sky. If a part of them stuck out of the shallow grave no one bothered to cover it. We buried one with his arm reaching out of his grave and left him that way beckoning grotesquely.

The possessions of the Japanese dead disappeared among souvenir hunters who quickly began their scavenging for pathetic mementos, some stained by the blood of friends and foe alike.

We ate our food near the enemy dead, drank coffee and chatted and argued. Some compared souvenirs, the size of gold teeth, photos of families, letters from wives and mothers, a bloody flag, a man's ear; oblivious to the proximity of their shallow graves. The flies that came to share our food were the same that fed on the corpses.

The possibility that soon one of those dead could be me, that I could possibly die, became very probable. Souvenirs were not important to me. My ass is the only souvenir I wanted to take home, and most shared that ambition for their own asses.

Each day took away more of our men so that we had suffered over two hundred percent in casualties. It was just a matter of time for the odds to catch up. If it were just a wound, an arm or a leg, or an eye I would have accept gladly, but I wanted to die in a clean bed. I did not want to loose my life here.

Death in youth meant a loss of thousands of potential days that make a life—loving, eating, working, vacationing, children, grandchildren sickness and health and then finally death. That made some sort of sense and was acceptable. The ending of a young life in this obscene way, however, was not acceptable to me. I wanted to experience a full, normal life,

Did Krup think of Wanda if he had a second or two before his brain died? Did he recall kisses and embraces in the car after the movies and the promises of continuing love? Or were his thoughts of his father and mother, like that boy in my foxhole calling, mama, mama?

Did he pray? He had no time. He did not hear nor see what killed him. There was no time, nor need, to put things and thoughts in order. It just abruptly ended.

There in the gore of his wounds, decay had already begun as God's nature had planned. He was dead and had become irrelevant. No one would ask his opinion of anything anymore. In time all living minds will have forgotten the dead, Polish-American boy. In a short time all would be forgotten.

"All this sound and fury", the wise poet said. "All this sound and fury would signify nothing."

Japanese diaries found on the island recorded the fear that they had and the fantastic plans they had concocted to escape and return home to friends and family. Some actually tried to journey over water in small boats to safe islands nearby, some tried to make it home. Many of the Japanese were young kids, poor kids. They were from all the main islands of Japan.

I imagined that among the dead enemy on the hill that morning one was a Private Toshito Yumushi from Hiroshima. Perhaps he had spent his last leave in his hometown just a few months ago before returning to Okinawa. He was only three hundred and sixty miles from home where his family prayed for him daily. In less than three months they would join him.

Toshito could have killed Krup last night. He could have been thinking how he could escape the island and the war by swimming back to Japan or to one of the small islands off shore were he could hide until the war was over.

He was trying to get back to own unit last night. Then he came out of his cave and started walking among the American foxholes not to kill, but to return to his comrades. He could have killed Krup by accident in all that confusion. Many were just killed by accident.

This could have happened.

They were both dead. No one will ever know what really had happened, not even we who were there. Perhaps Krup and Toshito were killed by friendly fire as so many others were. Now it did not matter.

Krup's mother and father attended the Greek Orthodox Church most mornings. The sunlight glinting on the golden domes gave them hope and courage. They probably were there that morning when their son was dead.

Krup and I had made an agreement to contact our families if one of us died. I was nineteen and took my time writing the letter which was very hard for me to do. I needed to put the words together and explain things to them.

They gave me Krup's .45 pistol. Others wanted it and tried to take it, but they knew I was his closest friend and gave it to me. The .45's were status symbols and treasured by Marines. It made us feel like a Hollywood hero, one of the cowboys.

I got to use that .45 only one time when several of us were standing on the side of a hill that was vulnerable to attack from a densely covered position a couple hundred yards away. Suddenly from a covering of brushes two young men in civilian clothing appeared and came towards me talking excitingly in Japanese. They were very young, about five feet five inches tall, and their were heads shaved.

When confronted by male civilians we were always apprehensive, not knowing if they were soldiers in civilian clothing. I could not tell if they were friendly or dangerous. They could be decoys and delaying us until their friends opened fire from the position across the way, or they could just be unlucky kids trapped among Marines.

I pulled Krup's .45 from my holster and pointed the gun at them shouting, "lift your hands". Then gestured with my arms upward to show them what I wanted.

They did not obey, either misunderstanding, or too frightened to do as I wanted.

I was scared shitless and excited as one of the men came very close to me jabbering and crying. I didn't know what to do but pointed the pistol inches from his face. Had they been armed I probably would have shot them. I'm not sure what I would have done.

I shouted for them to get their hands up, gesturing again, but they did not obey.

I was fearful that they were signaling for their friends to open fire on us. What the signal was I didn't know. If they were just acting, they were very good at it, crying and jabbering like idiots in terror.

The Marines I was with were occupied with other matters assuming I had my situation in control.

My two civilian 'prisoners' were both crying now and trying to explain to me something I did not understand and then one of them stumbled and began rolling down the very steep hill. The other, who I had my pistol on, turned and ran after his companion to rescue him or to escape, I don't know. He had chanced my shooting him in the face. But I was not going to shoot anyone in that situation. As they rolled and stumbled down the hill they were shouting and crying loudly and then disappeared into the dense brush near the bottom.

I don't think I would have shot those men if they were decoys, but I don't know. If there was an ambush I could not have saved myself. They would have killed me and the other Marines first. It was just an unexpected confrontation that could have ended worse than it did. The experience of pointing a pistol at a man's face and seeing the fear in his eyes was very distasteful to me and gave me no sense of power. I was glad that I did not have to look into the eyes of a human I had killed as I did into the eyes of the horse.

I could hear the warning advice, 'shoot first and ask questions later', offered me by many veterans who would suggest I had placed myself and my friends in jeopardy by hesitating to shoot these two boys. Perhaps they are right, but then, I was a very timid Marine.

◆   ◆   ◆

Dear Mr. And Mrs. Stanley Kruplowski
Conshohocken. Pennsylvania

My name is Lance and I was one of Dan's best friends. I was with Dan in Boot Camp and in New River and Boston Navy Yard. We were buddies and I was with him when he died. I promised Dan that I would get in touch with you when I could and tell you what happened.

Dan was hit while guarding our position one night and fought bravely and helped many of us guys to live. He loved you and he loved his country and I want you to know, I loved him too.

Yours truly, Lance

◆   ◆   ◆

What I really felt was that I was ashamed to be alive and able to write this useless letter to a mother and father who had lost their son, and his siblings who had lost their brother. But a promise is a promise, and I kept it even if I did not tell the story exactly as it happened. Civilians would never understand anyway. And who knows what happened? I didn't, and I was there.

◆   ◆   ◆

The day after Krup died we remained on the hill overlooking Naha. The grave registration people had done their jobs, collected dog tags, dug the graves, and identified the spot with the now ubiquitous white markers that were crowding the earth. The battlefield was returning to normal and we all sat around smoking and eating and shooting the bull. Naha had about sixty or seventy thousand people, many of whom were dead by now and the city was in ruins. Enemy resistance continued fanatically, forcing the brass with their maps to order continued bombardment of surrounding emplacements before continuing the frontal assault by the infantry.

A tall slim man smoking a pipe, followed by several younger men wearing officer emblems, was approaching. We were sitting in the same holes where the night before I had volunteered to vacate for the dying man from Massachusetts. After the previous night of death, this land, now witnessed our survival, our continuance.

Starting out as a gray, drizzly morning the day turned into sunlight with ocean shimmering in the distance. We were still alive and glad for it, surprised how time was actually trying to erase our nightmares. Survival makes one feel superior over the dead in some sad way. Survival is everything and can be improvised as you go. Death is nothing but a memory of sorrow that can't be changed.

The tall, old Marine, he was in his fifties, wearing a clean uniform approached us and I could see he was chatting with some of the guys as he approached our group and smiling. Those who followed were writing on pads. I don't know if they were writing stories or notes for a book or what. There sure as hell was nothing exciting going on then as there was last night. I could see by their uniforms that they had not spent the night in a foxhole. They were clean shaven and neat. Before the officer group reached us I could see the old Marine had stars on his collar. He was the commander of the Sixth Marine Division.

I was really doubting this whole war thing and thinking of ways to get out and save my ass. Seeing the General here, at what last night was the frontline, was supposed to be a moral boost for the troops who had almost lost their lives the night before. He expressed no sorrow for the men lost last night and no one told him that Krup had bought the farm along with many other kids. Generals don't like to hear about kids who bought farms while under their commands. He would not know Krup and of course, had no time for small talk about a dead Private. He would not know any of the other guys either. He was informed of the numbers. He knew numbers of dead and wounded, by the numbers, not by the names. It was his duty now to cheer the living, promise a few medals, and again prepare us to die. That was his job.

Enlisted men are always in awe of Generals, even if they swore at them behind their backs. There was too much power represented by those stars on his collar not to feel awed, especially when you are young. Those stars gave him the right to send men to die. There are fewer symbols more powerful that that.

I hated him, and wanted to tell him about Krup but, of course, I did not. I was afraid and embarrassed.

Someone asked the old Marine General, "When are we going in to take Naha, sir?"

"In a little while," the General answered. "We are going to let it get ripe like a plum, and then we'll pluck it." He made a delicate gesture with his fingers as though picking a fruit off a tree as he spoke the words.

By "get ripe" he meant that he was going to bombard the shit out of the place before he was going to send us in to take it, and no infantryman had a quarrel with that kind of logic. Too often, Generals sent men into battle before the enemy position was ripe for plucking. But looking down at Naha, now a heap of destruction, we wondered what there was left to destroy or pluck.

Then he smiled and put the pipe back in his mouth and moved on across the line boosting morale as he went. The young group of officers who followed smiled and continued taking notes. A photographer snapped photos as they went. Someday those photos would show up in scrap books and mementoes kept by people concerned with the General. Then, in time, they would all be forgotten like everything else. How I envied the General and the guys tagging along with him as they moved further and further away from this misery and returned to a nice clean area in the rear.

I took time during this lull to find LaFoo who was in another area. I had no problem locating him.

"Hi Louie," I called, when I saw his stocky figure in the distance.

He smiled and said, "Hi Poet."

"You know Krup got it last night," I told him.

"No shit," he said. "Sacre Bleu!"

"Yeah, no shit," I said.

He did not ask for details and I gave none. We both knew what had happened on that hill last night. That was all we said about Krup, each keeping our own thoughts.

An occasional enemy artillery started to test the range again, a round came towards us with a lazy, whooshing sound as though it lacked the power to fly. But still, if it hit nearby we could be dead. We had developed a habit during those days of ducking or at least bending from the waist a little and scrunching our necks on the approach of an enemy round until it passed over. Some of us still continued to dive into the nearest hole. But LaFoo continued talking to me as though nothing unusual was happening. He did not scrunch, bend, or flinch. He just continued talking as though there were no shells coming towards us. I was embarrass to jump into a foxhole, but I had to flinch and bend and scrunch my neck on the approach of every shell. He did not notice, or pretended not to notice my flinching. He just continued talking as though nothing was happening.

In this area there were still unburied dead enemy lying about. Two Marines were busy near us pulling gold teeth from the mouths of dead Japanese soldiers and one was cutting off a soldier's ear. A thin trickle of blood traced where the ear had been cut from the head. The man pulling teeth had a small, cloth pouch with a drawstring that he put the teeth in, and the other had a similar pouch for ears. The man pulling teeth used a pair of pliers and the point of his K-Bar knife to do his job. The other only need his knife for his task. Neither tried to protect their fingers from touching the dead men. When a tooth did not yield easily, the man would use his rifle but to smash the teeth lose, and then continue his extractions.

LaFoo and I looked at the two men briefly without comment. They chuckled and chatted as they collected.

LaFoo walked over to one of the Marines who was cutting another ear from the corpse and kicked the man in the back knocking him on the dead soldier. He did not say anything, not a word, and the stunned man looked up at LaFoo in surprise but did not complain. He recognized who had kicked him now and was not going to argue why. They remembered when he had shot the wounded civilian.

No one complained, no one asked questions. The look on Foo's face discouraged argument or questions. He had become one of those who we knew as being beyond reason or argument. One of those psychos, "you don't fuck with" when you're on the front line.

There were a few of us.

The men understood that they had annoyed LaFoo and left grumbling.

Personally, I could tolerate their actions, although very distasteful to me. Had the Japanese been alive and being tortured, I would have interfered without question.

I said nothing, and LaFoo remained silent too. I noticed that he had a bullet hole in his helmet. I asked him how it happened.

He smiled and said, "Yeah, that was a close one."

You could see he was proud of the close call.

The bullet had gone into the front of his helmet on an angle and then continued spinning around inside between the helmet and the helmet liner until it was spent. He smiled as he reached into his pocket and pulled out the bullet and held it up with two fingers as though performing a magicians trick. That was the only souvenir he wanted to take home.

The shells were coming over more frequently now but still over shooting our position. I was anxious to jump into a foxhole but could not do that while LaFoo was standing there calm and unconcerned. I made an excuse that I had to get back to my outfit.

A brief smile appeared and faded and he said, "Too bad about Krup, take care of yourself, Poet."

I said, "Yeah, you too, Foo, you too," and returned to my platoon where I could jump into a foxhole when the artillery started, without embarrassment.

Thinking that we had seen the inside of hell last night, we were surprised to hear that we were getting into position for one of the largest and most ferocious land battles of the Pacific war, the battle of Sugar Loaf Hill on Okinawa, according to The New York Times and other so called experts in these matters.

The previous night was only a prelude. Again the weather changed and a light rain fell. It would continue to rain again and would continue raining heavily, on and off for days, and with the rain came more artillery bombardment from the Japanese. They knew their days were ending and wanted to inflict the most pain possible. They were fighting on home ground, their families were only a few miles away. They knew American planes were bombing Tokyo and the other cities, they knew their families were suffering, they knew the importance of killing as many of us as they could.

The artillery, mortar and small arms fire targeted us as we moved to take a position at the foot of Sugar Loaf Hill. The confusion was beginning again but only earlier in the day. There was still plenty of daylight. Occasionally a scream or a moan would identify someone hit by bullet or shrapnel, sometimes there would be no moan if the shot was clean and got a man in the heart or head.

A man would be talking one minute and the next fall silent on his back with a clean bullet hole in his forehead. That's all she wrote and it was all over and final. One moment a man would be shouting orders, and the next lying in a pool of blood, dead.

It was a giant roulette wheel that kept spinning and falling on a number or color, and if it was yours, you were gone, all over, out. If you got a small nick, a few fingers blown off or a shoulder wound that did not take too much of you with it, you were envied.

"You lucky bastard, you're on your way home," we would tell the wounded man, wishing the wound were ours as he cried with pain..

We advanced to a new position where we were ordered to prepare foxholes again for the night. The rain began falling more heavily and it filled our foxholes. It had been raining off and on for days and the ground was saturated and turned to chocolate mud. We lay in the holes hugged up tightly holding our knees in a fetal position trying to take up as little space as possible. If one of those shells found our hole we would be gone. Just pieces of our bodies would litter the mud. If it missed, we survived for the next.

Each time we heard a shell coming our muscles would tense in expectation of being hit and then when the shell landed and burst we held our breath waiting for the shrapnel to cut through us even though we were in a hole. At times, on a close call, the burst would send a pile of dirt, mud, and rock over us and we trembled and twitched as the bits of debris rained down. Some shit in their pants, just a little, and I know I pissed in mine.

And again it happened and again and again. Occasionally a scream or calls for Corpsman told us someone had bought the farm. Million dollar wounds were not that easy to come by when artillery was shooting at you.

Now another shell came over us swishing and wobbling like a floppy wheel spinning in the air. It hit and there is no explosion. Is it delayed action? Will the timer run until reaching the set position and then explode? Our nerves and muscles are tense as we wait for the explosion which never came. A dud. Perhaps some Japanese girl in Nagasaki forgot to insert the fuse the right way while she was thinking about her boy friend. Maybe the timer was flawed. A dud, but it did damage to our nerves.

Surely the next one will land right on you and your buddy who is trembling so hard you can feel his whole body rocking like he was shivering from fever.

"What's the matter Buddy, why are you shivering?"

"I'm cold," he says.

And you understand. You are trembling too.

We were both trembling from fear.

You have to take a piss but dare not leave your hole and its is all wet with rain anyway. So you piss in your pants.

Your imagination tells you that the next one will be right on you. You hear it coming with that clean whistle spinning toward you and then it is silent before landing just like cutting a motor off in mid air. Just like a mosquito ready to dive. That brief moment of silence is an eternity and then it explodes and you are still alive after the fragments have been scattered and spent.

Lying there wet, cold and so afraid that you can barley talk, you think of home. You think of older men back home who did not have to fight, Mr. Smith, Mr. Jenkins, Mr. Grimes, men on your block who are laying in bed with their wives. Older men with children. Were they thinking of you? Did they know what we teenage boys were doing for them? You doubted it.

You have never had a girl for sex. Memories of the few dates in Boston with Phyllis warms you. You can feel her tongue in your mouth. You dream of doing it with so many girls and are sad and angry that you never will. So you dream of photos of movie stars in bathing suits. You are fighting and perhaps will die for all those old guys in bed with their wives, and your chance will never come.

Lying there I make a pact with God. I speak to Him, man to God. I know He is there and He is listening. He is my buddy and I am talking to him. God, you say, Buddy God, I love you God. If you get me out of this, bring me home to a girl I can love, then God, I promise you anything and everything. I believe in you, God, I was only kidding when I said I doubted. But you know my brain better than I do. I take everything back just please, oh, please get me out of this alive. I'll go to church, be a good boy, stop cursing, anything you want. Let me live God, please!!! Buddy?

The sergeant is yelling something in that grating voice of his, the Brooklyn, Italian, bastard. What was his name? Risso, Ricco, Americo? Italian guy. He was always shouting orders and now he is yelling something but it doesn't finish in his throat and his head has a tiny hole in the front and the helmet is knocked off his head. The sergeant is gone. No more shouting orders for him. Who will tell his mother?

Brief sorrow and continued fear, but no time for mourning, the next one may be yours.

He had an Italian name, I remember. Now a dead sergeant who had an Italian name. He left us so fast.

There was is an old Italian saying, brave men, like good wine, don't last long. The ugly, little joke runs through my brain now.

"A coward dies a thousand deaths, a brave dies only once." Oscar Wilde. How do the lines go? I can't remember them. I'm too afraid.

I was dying a thousand deaths. Each time I heard the shell scream, I died. Each time I heard a scream of pain, a cry for help, I died.

Am I a coward here, dying a thousand deaths, and the men torn by the last shell, heroes because they died? Are all brave men dead and we who live, or want to live, cowards?

Why have I lasted so long and why am I dying so often? Am I a brave man or a coward? God, old Buddy, are you listening? Will the next one be the one that I don't hear—the one that transforms me from coward to hero? The next one will take me to YOU and I don't want to see YOU yet.

There is that moist saccharine stench in the air again and it clogs my nose and coats it with that pungent, rotten sweetness. I can almost taste it. A cloth over my face does not defeat it. It enters my throat, clings there and sickens my brain to nausea. The smell of rotting human flesh returns.

The smell makes me think of the maggots I saw crawling out of the mouth of a young woman we came across earlier today. She had been stripped naked by a concussion that probably killed her and the maggots were crawling out of her mouth and vagina and some of the guys had laughs pushing a stick between her legs and pushed it into her vagina, in and out, in and out until the maggots oozed out of her mouth.

They made God angry and I will die for it.

It wasn't me God, I didn't do that.

I felt death in my heart and reminded God what I had promised, and pleaded to be spared. If not spared, I will be gone forever. I will be no more. To be no more. No more ice cold soda or ice cream, hot dogs and burgers, goodbye life. And the shells come, and come, and come, one after another, along with the rain and the stench of death. And I knew God was not listening and not interested in my game and never was. I had no pull with Him.

"We are going up the hill again," someone said, and like shadows we rise out of our holes and move forward foot by foot as the frightened enemy sitting in dry, dirty, waterless, rotten, foul, crowded caves try to kill us. Why are we doing this? Why are we out of our holes and moving towards death?

Someone ordered it. And we go. We go with an excruciating fear. And we kill and are killed and are battered back down the hill again.

We step on dead men on the way down and they are all ours. We are ordered to recover the dead and return up the hill to recover them. We recover parts and pieces and at times the whole dead man. Then later we recover rotted men who fall apart when lifted off the ground.

Orders to take this hill come from a safe and distant place. Somewhere where it is dry, clean and comfortable. Men talk and swear at each other by phone and look at maps and count numbers, and say, "go", by phone. This is relayed to the front line where the orders become personal. Sometimes, if the orders are too unreasonable or insane they are not followed, or executed in a manner that could save lives. The men who give the distant orders don't know exactly what is going on in each squad and platoon. They see the big picture of war, not the little picture of a group of men afraid of getting out of their holes to risk their lives.

Our regimental commander was a cautious man when ordered to send us into danger. He was relieved of duty for his caution. "Combat fatigue," they said. He was given a medal and sent home by the big General who visited us on the top of the Naha hill. I wished they would send me home too. The commanding officer probably saved many lives, but he was too cautious for the top brass. The top brass argues, he who hesitates is lost.

The wet, mud-clogged day turned into a black night with burning flares spitting bits of fire and crackling and smoking as they descended and sent a fake, yellow light over the torn land. We have become frightened demons climbing and descending from a hill known only by a number on military maps until death distinguished it with the name, Sugar Loaf.

I knew that God had disowned us and has refused to intercede. We have enlisted him to our cause without his permission and he is not answering our prayers.

I realized this. I decided, like God, not to participate in this madness any longer.

My brain said, this is enough.

I had eluded death, but death kept claiming all those around me, toying with me, until he would suddenly tap me on the shoulder when I least expected.

6

Combat Fatigue

The Marines and Army units fighting on Okinawa are experiencing the heaviest fighting of the Pacific War in their fight for the conquest of Sugar Loaf Hill, where a three day battle has caused casualties of over two hundred percent in some units. News report May 1945.

One in four world War II casualties was caused by combat fatigue. For those in lengthy intense fight the ratio was one in two. In the Pacific where combat fatigue was most prevalent 40 percent of the 1943 evacuations were, "mental." More than 26,000 psychiatric cases were report just from Okinawa. PBS The Mental Toll.

I would give all the gold in the world to stay alive.

I wanted to be alive the next day and all the thousands of tomorrows of a possible life. I wanted to stand up and say, hey, wait a minute, let's discus this thing. Let's talk about this very important thing we are doing here. We can talk this over and come up with a better solution. I had plans for my future: find a girl, finish high school, and the enjoyment of every mundane day of life. There was more to live for than die for.

What was the argument in the first place? Can't we discuss it again?

If we took a vote of the combatants I think peace would have won.

Emily Dickinson's poem intruded, "I did not wait for death but death waited for me..." over and over I repeated the words, "I did not wait for death, but death waited for me."

Did I remember the words correctly? Probably not.

I felt that some stranger was looking at me through his sights, or a haphazard mortar round was coming for me, the so called message of death with my name written on it. I could feel it in my bones, in my heart. I would be dead at nineteen and my family would cry. A few people in town would try to remember who I was and then give up. The man who killed me would never know how much I wanted to live.

My body would be gone. I would be no more.

Then in a few days it would all be forgotten. Where I died, and my friends died, and the enemy died there would be a parking lot for a shopping mall. Or perhaps here and there would be a park where families would come to play. They would laugh and have a refreshment and warn the kids to be careful while on the swings. The flowers would return and the trees would get taller. The sky would cheer this land where we crucified each other for our governments. The world would continue without us.

I stuck my foot over the edge of my foxhole hoping I would receive a good, honorable wound that would send me home. I aimed my rifle at my toes but could not pull the trigger. I had to be tested and tormented until my mind could not take it any longer. I wanted a wound of honor, a blood wound, shattered bone, any red badge of courage. I had reached my breaking point, my time to surrender.

I stood up so the whole world could see me under the surreal light of the flares. Men were shouting for me to "get down get down, you stupid, fucking bastard, get down."

We were all afraid and the fear made us angry and profane. But I was happy now and unafraid. For the first time in many days. I had surrendered and was ready to end my war. I was going to leave this madness. If both sides would join me, it would all be over. But they were too brave to surrender and did not know how.

I began to walked away from the insanity, exposing myself to death by standing while under heavy fire and going for a casual walk to the rear. I shuffled towards what I believed to be the safe, rear area dragging my rifle by its muzzle. I was headed where there was less noise, less pain and less fear. I kept walking. Nobody stopped me. I expected to feel the impact of a bullet in my back. It never came. I didn't care. I was escaping.

I did not know where I was going and did not care anymore. Some one grabbed me and was leading me away. The touch of the man's hand filled me with happiness. I had a chance to live.

A Corpsman had wrapped a piece of cloth around my arm which identified me as suffering an invisible wound, combat fatigue. The color of the cloth on my arm could have been yellow but I don't remember. At times Corpsmen wrote "psycho", "yellow" in their records when they tagged a man for combat fatigue. I walked to the rear with several others who had surrendered the fight.

As we walked I noticed that others along side me were gesturing and shouting wildly. Some were mumbling to themselves, manifesting combat fatigue in a more pathetic form. Other men were wounded and being carried to the rear on stretchers. There were a variety of wounds, lost legs, shattered arms, stomach and chest wounds, shattered faces. Those awake were shouting or screaming in pain, those unconscious moaned. Sometimes the morphine helped and sometimes not.

The smell of food being cooked, clean uniforms, clean bandages, the smell of medicine and lotions and even a whiff of perfume came to us as we were led to the rear. Somewhere there were women in those tents wearing perfume. Probably nurses. Just the idea of women being near calmed us. We knew it would be safe.

It seemed incredible that just a short distance behind the front line such a haven existed and I had reached it. I did not have to swim to Guam, which was one of my impossible plans.

I had reached a place where there were nurses with pressed uniforms and the sweet, clean scent of women. The nurses smiled at me and looked at the cloth around my arm and then told me to lie down on one of the cots. As soon as I dropped into the cot I went into another world where I was safe and happy. Had she injected my arm with a needle? Would someone clean me? I know that there was a foul smell about me of piss and shit and blood.

They left me in a strange sleep for a long time. In the distance I could hear very faintly the echoes of artillery explosions, but it was far away and it lulled me into a deep sleep. It was more like a lullaby now that I knew I was safe.

I slept for a long time. When I awoke a young doctor asked me how I felt and did I want something to eat. I said yes.

There were several other men in the tent with me and none of them showed any sign of injury. Everyone was well groomed and clean. Everyone smelled good. They had removed my foul dungarees and boots. Someone had wiped me with disinfectants. I smelled like a clean urinal.

A tray of food was brought to me by a young kid about my own age, and it smelled like something I never smelled before. It was gloriously fragrant and enticing. It was warm. Actually hot food that I had never expected to taste again.

When I put a forkful of it into my mouth I could not swallow. I had the vision of eating human flesh, bits of human parts, a finger, a piece of brain swarming with maggots. It clogged in my throat and would not be coaxed down completely, and suddenly the little that I swallowed came bursting out of my mouth smelling to me like rotted flesh. I dropped the food tray to the floor and retched with the taste of decay. No one asked me what was the matter and even if they did I had no answer. They were familiar with this problem.

I kept smelling beautiful hot food all around me but was not hungry. I kept smelling perfume and clean uniforms and sheets and all I wanted to do is to disappear and become invisible. I wanted desperately to be forgotten and disappear so they would not end my dream. This haven was only temporary, I knew, and they would soon trick me into going back. The fear of being returned to the front lines frightened me so badly that I refused to contemplate it. When I did, I began to tremble.

Most of the other guys in my tent did not say much. All young kids, they looked unhurt except the distorted muscles of their faces that showed where fear had creased a furtive look of a trapped animal. We were all little animals afraid of being abused. We did not talk. We did not trust each other, and we were ashamed of being there without wounds that bled. Most of us were there for the same reason. We suffered combat fatigue. But a few had body wounds and were bandaged.

I envied their wounds, wishing that I had the bandaged arm or leg, wishing even to having lost an arm or leg. That would have been a good reason for being here. I envied their good fortune.

The wounded did not show any signs of fear in their eyes. They were the only ones who spoke a little. They even smiled and were at ease with the nurses. When one of them without malice asked why I was there in the tent with the others. I answered, "I'm sick."

The words stuck in my throat like the hot food that would not pass into my stomach. I felt that I really had nothing wrong with me, and I was ashamed being in a tent with wounded men.

After another night of sedated sleep, a hot shower, and a cup of coffee my body almost returned to its former teenage quality. The closeness and the smiles of a young nurse helped to clear my wounded mind even more.

This was the prescribed treatment for combat fatigue, a few days of rest, clean surroundings, food and safety, and perfumed nurses. Officers were treated the same but only in more remote areas. I never saw a combat fatigued officer. That would not be good for morale. Officers are not supposed to fatigue, and probably, if they did, were not returned to fight too quickly, if ever.

They kept enlisted men closer to the front to ensure that they would not get used to being too far away from the horror to which they would be quickly returned. Getting too accustomed to safety and sanity so close the front is not good for infantrymen. It allows them to compare the unjust dissimilarity and demoralizes them further.

I wanted something more tangibly wrong with me so the doctors could keep me hospitalized for a few more days. I prayed for a fever, an infection. I could place some brown soap under my armpits to raise my body temperature. Someone had told me that it worked. I tried, and it did not. I put the tip of my cigarette on the base of the thermometer to raise the temperature for the nurse to read. It burst.

I told the nurse, "It broke"

"So I see," she said.

She knew why. Others had done the same.

The next night there was fresh meat and creamy sauce, fresh biscuits, apple pie and coffee, and all the milk you could drink. Cold soft, sweet milk. Now I ate, and kept it where it belonged. After dinner I walked around the hospital area and I could hear music coming from one of the large tents. A radio or phonograph playing. Nurses and medical men in uniform were coming in and out of the tents chatting and laughing.

I never wanted to leave this place.

I knew that these people did important work in caring for the wounded and that they had to have relaxation, but they could not imagine what is was just a short distance forward at the front line. I envied them, and knew that I was not qualified to be with them here in their safe world. I didn't care. I did not want to reason logically. I just did not want to return to that hell I escaped from just because I was only a infantryman. I promised myself that someday, if I lived, I would qualify myself to live in their world too.

Several days later two young doctors came to my bed and started to ask questions. I knew my time was running out and soon they would be doing their duty to get me back up there.

"What happened to you?", asked the slim, young doctor, a psychiatrist, blond, fair skinned blue eyes. Handsome. He was the guy in high school who got all the girls and wore the beautiful sweaters with varsity letters to football games. He was the guy who was class president or treasurer. He was a winner and it figured. I knew he was the opposite of me, but I wanted to live as much as he did.

I told him what happened to me in broad terms. To him there was no uniqueness in my tale. He had heard all those stories before. I saw no compassion in his face. The other doctor who was with him looked sad. They were in their late twenties or early thirties perhaps. They were old men to me, and an ocean of social differences separated us.

I told them about the blood and the death and the fear.

"Don't you want to go back to your outfit?" Don't you want to be with your buddies?"

They were trying to embarrass me. They were not really listening to me.

Why don't you go see my buddies, I thought. Why don't you spend a few days up there and then ask me that question. Most of "my buddies" were dead or wounded. There were only strangers up there. Replacements who I never met before, and a trapped, fanatical and frightened enemy.

"No", I said, "I want to stay here."

I was not a good actor to fake combat fatigue. I could not fake screaming, trembling or insanity. I did not envy those who did, if there were any, but I wished I had been more apparently unstable.

If I was meant to die here, I thought, I wanted everyone to know it, all my friends and teachers back home, and not go obscurely like an old horse. I wanted an audience for such an important event in my life, but more importantly, I wanted to live.

"You're not a coward, are you? You're not yellow. Are you yellow?"

Sticks and stones, I thought. "Coward, Yellow." They are goading me. But still the words stung. The name calling perhaps had some therapeutic value in their practice.

"I don't know," I said, "I don't know what a coward is. I know that I was scared to death of being shot or blown up in a foxhole."

I was ashamed to mention Krup and the names of others who died, using them as the reason for my being there. They did not care anyway, and to bring those names to this place would be irreverent. To me those were special names that should not reach callous ears. Those names belonged only to me and the others who loved them.

I was hurt that they insinuated that I was yellow. We are conditioned from childhood to shame if we are described by that color. But this was no longer football games or even war games. Yellow, green or blue, I just wanted to stay alive.

"Let me live," I wanted to beg and lose my pride, but could not.

I had done some brave, stupid and timid things on this island. I did not feel I had to explain my courage to noncombatant men in clean uniforms who smelled of shaving lotion.

I know I wanted to be safe and clean rather than a sacrificial animal, joining the countless millions who went before me.

"Well, you can't stay here, you have to go back in a couple of days. Your buddies are counting on you. This place is for wounded men." The handsome, young doctor passed sentence on me as he was instructed to by someone up the line, or more likely, he was just following the rules and regulations of his profession. Going by the book

It was his job to get me back on the front lines. I understood that. He didn't care personally about my fear. He had a job to do and believed it was right. His orders were to get combat fatigue cases back to the front as soon as possible unless they were severe. How they determined degree of severity I don't know and it probably varied from time to time depending the need for men at the front.

In any case, he was ordering me to return to die.

I hated him for asking me those questions about being a coward and being yellow. I wanted to see his ass up there for one hour, then we'd see who was a coward. I wanted him to understand why I was so afraid of going back and he was not interested. He had his job to do.

I realized that socially, economically, and intellectually I belonged at the front. That was my destiny in life when war came as it was my father's and grandfather's. We are a line of people who are used up in wars. Cannon fodder, food for cannons. And we face our counterparts on the enemy side. The losers fighting losers.

I would have to save myself by my wits.

At that point I did not know whether I could go back. My one rifle was not important, I felt. But that was not the point. It was not only my rifle. There were thousands of rifles that the owners wanted to renounce, and that could not be permitted. No government could permit that. If everyone disowned their rifles, there could be no war.

We had been duped by propaganda movies about the glorious war and the need to join up. I did, and now I felt I had done more than my share.

I felt like a fool remembering how I sat through those war movies getting goose bumps on my teenage skin. I remembered my father telling me it was all a fake. He had been in the first world war and did not enjoy war movies. Now I understood what he meant. By fake, he meant they were not honest. I had to find my own way to out fox these bastards and survive. That was the only answer, the only victory, survival.

I thought of the millions of mothers and fathers who had seen governments send their boys to war knowing the horror that awaited them but could not speak it. I remembered my father crying as he looked up at me sitting in the bus waiting to take me away to Boot Camp. He knew what was waiting at the end of the ride.

The psychiatrists left me to think my thoughts and knew they had implanted the fact that I would be returning to the front. I would have no choice. They were sending me back.

◆   ◆   ◆

During the night they shipped in another load of wounded. The trapped enemy was being squeezed into a smaller and smaller position from which they fought like frightened animals and our casualties rose. Whenever battles accelerate, combat fatigue casualties also increase, and Division Headquarters ordered the medical units to be more strict in accepting combat fatigue cases. How they followed that order I don't know. Did they leave men on the line until they went insane?

I heard them rearranging the beds during the night. Men were moaning and there was no attempt to keep things quiet. In the morning I saw one of the men on other side of the large tent who looked familiar. He was bandaged and there was red blood showing through the bandaged leg which was amputated above the knee. It was Jimmy Long.

I felt like shit seeing him there without a leg and me with nothing physically wrong. I hesitated before approaching him, but we were old buddies, and I had to talk to him.

His bunk was neater than all the others which were in fine condition but somehow JD had the nurses put everything around him in order. I smiled at that. Even with a serious wound JD presented himself in a military manner.

I remembered that several days ago I had volunteered to help him carry ammunition across an open field under sniper fire as a gesture of our friendship. I was proud of that and knew that JD remembered. It was something I did with no ulterior motive other than seeing expression of thanks in a friends' eyes.

"JD, old buddy," I called to him in feigned lightness, and he turned at the sound of my voice, surprised to hear it here in the hospital.

"Lance," he shouted in surprise. "What the hell are you doing here? Were you wounded too?"

He didn't wait for an answer and I did not give one.

"When did you get hit," I asked.

"Several days ago, I think. It's hard for me to remembered the days."

"Yeah, I know what you mean. Same for me too."

"It looks like you'll be going home soon," I said stupidly.

"Yeah."

"Are you feeling okay. Do you have any pain?"

"No," he said. "They are giving me something to kill it."

"So what's with you, Lance? Why are you here?"

The words almost stuck in my throat, "I cracked up," I said.

"Yeah? No shit? A lot of guys were cracking up when I got hit. Are they sending you home?"

He showed no resentment that I was whole and he was without a leg. He did not question that I cracked up and took it for granted that it could occur.

"No," I said, feeling better that I could tell him I was going back and only needed a rest.

"I wish they would send you home, too. Everybody should go home from this friggin war," he said.

Then he turned his head. He had tears in his eyes.

I grabbed his hand and said, "I'm sorry you got hit, JD, real sorry."

He said, "I know."

He did know, and he knew too, that I envied him his wound.

Then he told me that he had heard that Karnes was also wounded but did not know the details.

"You know how these things are," JD said, "I only got part of the story."

"He got hit before I did," JD said

My heart was pained with this news about Lee in addition to the sight of JD with one leg. It seemed that each day brought us another sorrow of friends killed or wounded. Now Karnes, too. I remembered that night I stood guard with him when he held his fire to save innocent people. It seemed a hundred years ago.

"He must have been wounded pretty bad because they shipped him to the USS Comfort hospital ship," said JD, remembering another bit of information.

I felt good about that because the Comfort was a fine hospital ship with the best of medical equipment and was painted brightly like a cruise ship, but had red crosses painted on her to indicate her purpose. It was a good, safe place for Karnes to be for medical attention.

JD was falling off to sleep and I left him.

When I returned for another visit later in the day he was gone. They had transferred him, and that is all I knew.

His million dollar wound cost him one half a leg at the knee and crippled the other for years until he got enough strength to use it.

The next day I was discharged from the hospital and they gave me a jeep ride towards the front along a road where a large group of men were working. The driver was not going to take me right to the fighting front. In fact, they did not know where the actual fighting was.

"You can find your unit from here," he said "Some of these guys will get you there, and good luck."

He knew I needed it and perhaps was a little embarrassed that he was going back towards the rear.

"Good luck", they called as the sped away.

I had no paper work to show where I had been or where I was supposed to be going. I was just a lone infantryman on the road looking for his outfit that was up front fighting. Somewhere.

I was still far from the front. I could feel it in easy going activity around me. This was the rear echelon.

Infantrymen always kidded rear echelon personnel for having it easy. We all wished we were rear echelon. The quartermaster people, headquarters company, and a variety of support units were in the rear echelon. More troops were in the rear echelon than were at the front lines with a ratio of ten to one. The personnel back here were those who manned the long range artillery, Seabees, engineers, military police, quartermaster, headquarters and other lucky guys who had a bigger talent than just carrying a gun.

I walked slowly, talking to men along the way asking for my unit and no one knew exactly where it was. They pointed toward the front vaguely. When night fell I joined a group of men in a quartermaster unit and told them I was on my way back to the front. They understood my reluctance and seemed embarrassed knowing the differences of our missions. They allowed me to stay with them for a while.

"Don't hurry," they said "there is plenty of time to get back there." They knew each day of survival was important.

They knew I was not in any hurry and they were regular guys, not eager like the psychiatrists to get me back. We listened to the radio every night and that's when I heard that the USS Comfort had been hit by a kamikaze. Karnes was on board, I knew, and later found out he was killed. I knew there was no Chevra Kadisha for him, and wondered where his grave was, land or sea. I never found out. I had failed to guard his body until his soul had left it as I had promised.

I wondered if he had time at least to say that prayer he told me about, "Blessed are you our G-d creator of time and space who enriches our lives with holiness commanding us to wrap ourselves in the tallit." I wondered if the four cornered poncho would have served as a substitute tallit. Would strict religious laws bend a little in times like these for a young man who was searching his way to G-d.?

I spent more time with my rear echelon friends before I continued the search for my outfit. There was no set plan or any communications about my movements, so I took my time as I continued my reluctant journey to the end of the last battle of the war.

We were no longer under enemy shell fire so I knew it was getting near the end. Everyone knew it. Their big guns had been destroyed and now all that remained for the overmatched, out-supplied and over whelmed Japanese was to surrender or die.

They had been pushed to the end of the island which was a third the size of Rhode Island, 60 miles long and about 13 miles wide. Even now, before the official end of the battle this island was being prepared as a huge platform to launch the invasion of Japan. In the rear area the Seabees and Army Engineers were bull-dozing the land into large runways to accommodate our bombers.

When I reached my unit, it was a bright, beautiful, sunny day. Most of the men I had known were gone. It was like joining a platoon of strangers. Only one or two remembered me. The platoon leader was new and did not know who I was and was not expecting me. I had no written orders to give him. The medical people only had put me on a jeep and told me to get back.

One guy who recognized me was a chubby little Marine we called Willy. He was short, and soft, and comically participated in our adventures, but he had remained with the platoon from beginning to end escaping wounds, insanity and death.

Willy knew I had been evacuated for combat fatigue and to him that meant I was a little crazy.

Willy was the butt of many jokes which I now realized served as a safety valve for our many precarious days. He waved to me as I approached and was on his way to the slit trench nearby with an handful of toilet paper. I remember he had no jacket and his soft, white skin seemed incongruous after all he had been through. He pulled down his pants after straddling the ditch, and I got the idea to play a last joke on him.

I unscrewed the top of a grenade and emptied the powder charge to render it harmless, just as the DI had done on Parris Island. Only the primer powder was in place.

I pulled the grenade pin and began screaming, "I'm going nuts. I'm cracking up again."

Willy looked at me in horror.

I then released the handle of the grenade and rolled it smoking, towards Willy who was in the middle of his defecation. Willy saw the smoking grenade rolling towards him, and thinking I had cracked up "again", left his straddle position and began to run with his pants down until he fell to the ground with his hands over his head. The grenade fizzled out and we all laughed at another joke on poor

Willy who sheepishly got to his feet smiling, promising to get even with me some day.

While I played my adolescent prank, Japanese, and civilian men, women and children not far away, were being killed or committing suicide.

We were several hundred yards from the last killing which we were watching as spectators from a high position overlooking a long plain with tall growing grass and reeds. A lingering coup de grace of the Japanese was being administered by our overwhelmingly superior force. The battle was almost over. We could see the last slaughter of the enemy before our eyes like a sad execution.

During this horrible day for the Japanese, just after my prank on Willy, I met an old school chum, Freddy Bav, who was in the First Marines. He was a sports star at Lodi High School and in our sand lot games, too. He told me that I had joined the Marines because of him, trying to match his ability. He was partly right. I could not equal him on the sport field and failed again in the Marines.

We shook hands and I told him to be careful, "it is almost over."

He smiled, but I don't think he knew what I meant. He was lucky enough to come back alive, however, and live a full life.

There was little land remaining for the enemy to fight from. The cliffs at the southern end of the island had a massive beehive of caves used for a last stand. They were all huddled in those putrid, almost airless caves waiting to die. Even the civilians families who were caught in the caves with the soldiers knew it was nearing the end and they would join many soldiers in committing suicide before it was all over.

At that time, being so young, I could not fathom, the tremendous horror those people endured. They were trapped with their children while we trying to shoot and burn them to death, and the Japanese were urging them to commit suicide by jumping off the cliffs or exploding grenades against their bodies.

The Americans turned on loud speakers and asked them to surrender and not be afraid. Some fortunate ones were able to surrender but most could not.

Some came out and were shot by their own men or by Marines. Some chose to come out and blow themselves up with explosive charges around their bellies.

The soldiers looked so frightened, small, and sadly comical, not like haughty Samurai. Half naked, they ran out of the caves into the open and blew themselves up in front of us as a last display of defiance, or allegiance to their Emperor. Some pulled the detonators at the mouth of the caves and were gone. Others ran half naked into the high grass trying to escape but were gunned down like small, defenseless game animals by Marines no longer in jeopardy. It all played before our eyes like the sad ending of a badly made B movie. To me, there was not glory here. Thankfully, no one ran to place the flag on the top of that last hill.

Many civilians, including children, who were with them committed suicide by jumping off the high cliffs to the rocks below. Top officers committed suicide in accordance with their ancient and out dated traditions. But somehow over 6,000 managed to surrender according to some of the records after the war.

The prisoners were herded into small corals and stripped of their clothing except for some type of loin cloth wrapped around their skinny bodies. They assumed a squatting position that was common in Asia, sitting on their heels with bended knees and feet flat on the ground. All looked undernourished, tired, hungry, and afraid. They gazed straight ahead with a furtive, animal stare in anticipation of some punishment.

In one of the caves eighty five young student nurses where killed by American troops. Today it is a shrine visited by many Japanese, its memorial plaque points out that the girls were killed by the Americans. It is called the Cave of the Virgins. It is a tourist site today for Japanese. I did not know about it until later.

The enemy soldiers were mostly just ordinary men, poor men. Not all of them had raped and murdered civilians in China just as not all Marines had not raped and murdered civilians on this island. I don't know if they were more barbaric than those buddies who smashed dead mouths to extract gold teeth or cut off ears as mementos, or killed old horses out of boredom. I don't know if one race of men is any more brutal than another but I believe not. It depends on many circumstances, the level of brutality a human can achieve.

The dead civilians were innocent and painful sacrifices.

I record a lot of my own terror here and the terror of the combatants on both sides because I knew these fears best. I saw that fear personally on both sides. However, the terror and suffering of civilians goes mostly unrecorded. One can only imagine what it was like for them. The killing and wounding of children, the young nurses, old men and women were cruel tragedies that have been mostly forgotten.

Those of us who surrendered to the horror would question ourselves morally for the rest of our lives. Having been part of a society that celebrates heroes on the sports field, and battlefield, where winning is everything, we hesitate to suggest otherwise. We have been indoctrinated to accept the traditional depiction of war as lied about and romanticized in television, movies, and novels, but more and more we are learning to question.

◆   ◆   ◆

During this battle, as in most battles, the high ranking officers, politicians and amateur experts argued about the conduct of the campaign. The commanding Army General who was killed had been criticized continuously for his military decisions. The arguments evaluating military maneuvers continued long after the campaign and probably will continue for years to come when history buffs become interested in this little battleground.

The evaluation of the campaign by the tall, publicity enamored, Army General with the corncob pipe and sunglasses, was that there was no reason to seize the southern end of the island, (where most of the casualties occurred), after the enemy had been contained there. He said we had enough anchorages and airfields on the northern section for the invasion of Japan. He felt that the cornered Japanese on the island would have 'died on the vine'.

Sadder still were the evaluations of "experts" who said the battle was superfluous and did nothing to end the war and could have been avoided.

I don't care much for Generals who are politically and professionally ambitious and take the opportunities presented by disasters, that take the lives of young men and innocent people, to advance their egos. They are of an ilk, educated as technicians, not poets. They criticized each other constantly as Monday morning quarterbacks, proving that the technology they are taught, is flawed.

◆   ◆   ◆

I was alive and that was all that mattered to me. I chose not to be hypocritical and puff my chest in pride for being a Marine. I was just an ordinary kid afraid of being killed and lucky to survive. I learned that under enough stress, I would break down.

I tried to comfort myself by rationalizing that there were thousands more like me, but found no solace in the crowd. And still I hear the voice of the young psychiatrist asking me, "Are you a coward?"

7

Guam, China, Home

The Marine invasion force on Guam training to assault Kyushu, Japan heard the news of the Japanese surrender last night and the island went wild with joy. It was a reprieve from imminent peril to their lives. Over one million casualties were expected in the invasion of Japan. News item August 1945.

Much of the news of Okinawa, the last Pacific battle of the war, was pushed off the front pages of American newspapers by the news of the President Roosevelt's death on April 12 and the end of war in Europe in May. For once the Marines did not capture the big headlines. Generals depend on headlines for future recognition and promotion, but for the infantry grunt, getting home was the prime goal.

When the ships from Okinawa landed on Guam after the battle in June 1945, thousands of sea bags were unloaded, some of which belonged to Marines who had been killed, wounded or missing. The sea bags were full of clothing and other things desperately needed by the Guamanians. The canvas sea bags were loaded on trucks and transported to an open area on the island where they were bull-dozed into large piles, drenched with gasoline and set afire.

Many Guamanians circled the burning sea bags waiting for the fire to die down enough for them to retrieve a charred bag and its contents, perhaps a pair of shoes or a blanket. For the most part they were unsuccessful and what they salvaged was partially burned and not useable. They wondered why the Americans would do such a thing. Why would they rather destroy useful material rather than give it to needy civilians who had been their allies during the war. For many years this alienated many islanders, but they had no political power to change things.

I remember walking along a little dirt on Guam with a few friends on one summer day in June 1945 and hearing the voices of children who were singing in a distant school. The children's voices with an island accent lent an extra gaiety to the beautiful day. The music and the words were so haunting that I remembered parts of it for many years. These people had been living under Japanese rule since they occupied the island early in the war. During that time, this song had been written and sung.

"Oh Sam, Sam, my dear Uncle Sam won't you please come back to Guam."

The children sang this refrain over and over along with other segments I have forgotten.

Uncle Sam had returned but was not sharing sea bags and many other items with the people. Perhaps there was a reason for burning the sea bags because some belonged to Marines who had died and many personal items were in the bags. But these people desperately needed shoes and clothing and anything that makes life easier like tooth brushes, paste, soap, toilet paper. etc. The islanders clutching at burning canvas sea bags retrieved from the fire did not understand the reasoning.

Soon there would be an endless stockpile of military equipment, including tents, trucks, planes, artillery, ammunition, medical supplies, canned food, and everything that keeps troops in war, stored on this tropical island. It would be preserved for a short time and then rot. The tropical weather and the salt of the sea would reduce most items into nothing.

Duty on Guam in June and July of 1945 consisted of general duties without any dramatic marches or training for landings. This was surprising to us because the next big step would be landing on Japan's main islands. The prospect of the coming invasion of Japan disturbed our sleep with nightmares. My mind was scheming plans to avoid death in Japan.

I remember the Red Cross canteen that was set up for us just off base. It had a large map cut out from some magazine showing Japan and the planned invasion, hanging on one wall. The map identified the various units that would participate and where they were expected to land. Our Division was graphically included at the end of an arrow with its point in Kyushu. I shivered at the thought. How was I going to avoid that one? The Japanese would be so infuriated by an invasion they would fight like madmen. Over a million of us would be killed, according to some reports. I hated the sight of that map.

But we loved the sight of the American Red Cross women who manned the canteen wearing clean uniforms and smiling at us. They knew we were heroes just returned from war. Oh, yeah.

For the enlisted man it was his reward just to look at the pretty women and don't touch or even leer. Most of us were still teenagers and the women were in their twenties or thirties, some older. One of our group was an older guy and married, and we thought it would be a good idea to have him approach one of the younger woman and ask her for a date. He was a good looking guy and about the same age as the young Red Cross woman.

At first he was against the idea but we promised to provide a jeep for the planned date, and also chipped in over a hundred dollars to entice the women with gifts. He agreed to try.

It took him several days to get the courage and the right time. It was difficult to talk to Red Cross women with all the men around. The men were just glad to be near them and smell perfume again. We gazed, salivated and fantasized our sexual orgies.

If our candidate to seduce the Red Cross woman succeeded, our reward would have been vicarious, proxy sex. We waited to witness his attempted seduction one afternoon when the young lady was free from the usual crowd around her. From a distance we tried to look unconcerned, pretending to read magazines, but peeked to see what was happening.

We could see them both laughing and she shaking her head, no. He was blushing and looked handsome and persistent. Would he continue and win the day for us? After a few minutes, she still shook her head, no, and he shrugged his shoulders in defeat.

The rejection rejected us all. We blamed his being an enlisted man as the reason for the rejection.

"If you had bars on your collar you would be sleeping with her tonight," we tried to bolster the rejected lover.

"Everybody knows the Red Cross women are officer pussy anyway," we continued the old refrain that repeated itself across the Pacific with little veracity.

There were probably hundreds of times that these young women were propositioned during their tour of duty. The men they met often wanted more than doughnuts and coffee to cheer them up.

We all lived in rows of tents as usual, that had to withstand the heavy tropical rains of the South Pacific. When that rain came in sheets rather than drops it saturated the tent canvas so much that it leaked through. Not even on Okinawa did we see rain like that. The only difference was that Guam had sand to absorb the water instead of dirt. However, the area around the tents, after these deluges, would be flooded. Once again we were in a place that never got dry. Jungle sores abounded and the smell of medicated powder and lotions permeated all the tents.

June passed into July and then into August. Each day more boring than the preceding. There was little to do other than patiently wait for the dreaded invasion of Japan.

I still had the .45 pistol that belonged to Krup but it was getting more and more difficult to keep. The officers called inspections almost on a daily basis to check our tents for any weapons we were not supposed to have. I was running out of places to hide the pistol. The last hiding place I tried was in a sand hole outside our tent. I wrapped the pistol in plastic and buried it. As the days went by I forgot exactly where the hole was and had difficulty retrieving it.

Finally I gave it up when an officer offered me several bottles of whiskey for it. Officers were permit to have a .45 pistol and enlisted men were not unless we were in combat.

It was just a matter of time before it would be confiscated anyway. I did not drink whisky then but several of my buddies did and they drained the bottles quickly. Krup would have understood.

I found myself on KP again for some infraction of minor importance and I turned KP into an opportunity to requisition powdered ice cream and other supplies for my tent mates. This was a special treat because the powdered ice cream when mixed with water could pass for a liquid cream which resembled the real thing if you did not have a discriminating palate. My friends appreciated the gift and all the others I was able to provide during my KP duty.

The boring days on Guam came to end one day in August. There was an excitement in the air and shouting along tent rows. Words got through to my ears in bits of sentences. "Over, no landing, bomb. No Japan, It's over."

Laughter and singing and shouting accompanied the scene of men hugging, shaking hands, and slapping each other on the back. The war was over. We had dropped the Atomic Bomb. Whatever that was. What a sweet little sentence, the war was over. The words sounded like a beautiful poetic lyric. The war was over. We repeated it over and over for the sheer joy of the sound. They were words we thought we would never hear.

The news on following days explained more and more, and then there was another bomb, and it was really over. The joy. We were going to live our lives and not be killed in Japan.

The bombs had killed over two hundred thousand people, but had supposedly saved millions if Japan was invaded. We accepted it. Wanted to believe it desperately and were glad.

Within a few days, units of Marines on Guam were already on their way to China to accept the Japanese surrender there, and to keep the Communists from taking the seacoast cities of China. A few Marines including me were left on Guam to perform clean up details.

Work details were disassembling tents, and packing weapons coated with creosote for preservation. There were thousands of tents that had to be dismantled and stored away or burned. In time all our efforts were to no purpose, for the elements soon began to eat away the canvas tents as well as the metal of tanks, vehicles, planes and everything else on this earth that can deteriorate back into it. In this part of the world you learned quickly how material things soon are reduced to nothing.

For almost two months we labored under the heat of the tropical sun taking down tents, folding them and packing them into squares packages that could be handled more easily. My insubordination had once again placed me in a uncomfortable position. The good Marines were already in China enjoying girls and a bit of freedom while we on shit details were doing donkey work in the jungles.

When our job was done on Guam we were ordered to rejoined our outfits in China.

◆　　　◆　　　◆

The slow moving transport had finally reached the port of Tsingtao on the tip of the Shantung peninsula across from the islands of Japan. We had sailed from Guam after securing our camp sites and now the pilot was directing the ship into its berth as swarms of Chinese performed various functions on the docks and along the roads. This was the first foreign country I had seen in my life. China with all its mystery, and romance. All the movies I had seen came back to remind me about this strange and wonderful land. Charlie Chan, Marco Polo, The Good Earth; movies, movies always were our reference points.

We boarded trucks that took us through the city streets towards Shantung University where our regiment was stationed. I felt like we were in hostile territory. We were among Asians still. We carried our full packs and our weapons were loaded. Almost everyone was Chinese and I felt disoriented and uneasy as our trucks made their way through streets crowded with rickshaw traffic and vendors.

Some of the rickshaws were carrying big, well fed Marines which I thought ridiculous. I promised myself I would never ride on a rickshaw. The idea that a man pulled another man around like an animal in that degrading manner was very distasteful to me. However, after several weeks in the country I became accustomed to it. The whole experience, sights, smells, sounds, were exciting, disturbing and wonderful to me.

In the countryside some remaining Japanese military personnel were still being rounded up for return to Japan. There were also some civilian Japanese families in the city waiting for deportation and their situation was precarious. They never knew when some trigger happy patrol would come upon them during the night and kill them all. Patrols went out every night to keep order in the city and we often entered Japanese homes and were invited in by the occupants who offered us hospitality but with an underlying fear. They were ultra hospitable but not with genuine friendship. Peace was very new.

Shantung University consisted of a series of brick and stone buildings, some four stories high, that formed a square around a huge court yard. These building were protected by a high brick wall which was wide enough for men to walk on for guard duty. Two gates guarded the university, the main gate through which most traffic passed to the business district, and the rear gate, a smaller one, which led to the north side of the university towards rural section of the city.

Our truck convoy entered the main gate and deposited us at the main building where we got directions to our rooms. They had been classrooms, and dormitories. My room on the second floor had six men assigned to it. There was no central heating and winter was just beginning in that part of the world which could get very cold when the Mongolian winds started pushing through.

The whole floor smelled of fried eggs and I soon saw why. There was a frying pan with a half dozen eggs on a small kerosene stove in my room. Against one corner of the room hundreds of empty egg shells formed a pyramid. Our fondness for fresh eggs had been satisfied by duty here, and inspections had obviously been relaxed.

The toilets were at the basement level where showers were erected to accommodate a large group of men. The water was of questionable reliability and often changed from warm to ice cold without warning and with considerable pain to the bathers, but we were young.

A favorite room of mine in the University was the large third floor library overlooking the court yard. I spent many hours there reading and looking into the yard below, sipping the wonderful Tsingtao beer. This beer was made from a German brew recipe left by those who had concessions in this city before the Boxer Rebellion. The beer would become world renown in a few years. In those days with the shortage of glass, the beer was bottled in a variety of bottles of all shapes, colors and sizes. Milk bottles, old Coke bottles and large soda bottles were used to bottle the brew. The bottles were often corked with wax, but the beer was excellent and inexpensive.

Looking down into the courtyard library after being in China only a few days I saw a strange gathering of men below. The bugle call had summoned us to fall out but I took my time watching what was happening in the court yard below.

The cold November wind swirled into the courtyard unhampered by any shielding structure as streams of Marines poured out of the brick buildings. They were all dressed in parts of uniforms, fatigues, dress greens and some with over-coats. They formed several long lines facing a group of men who sat at a table at its head. These men were taking notes and peering at the crotches of the man standing before them.

"Short Arm inspection", someone called out, and the word was passed room to room and building to building. Pass the word, "Short arm inspection, short arm inspection, short arm inspection."

I knew about short arm inspections and participated in one or two since join-ing the Corps but I never saw one forming like this.

There were five, and then six lines of men shuffling along toward the Corps-man sitting on a chair that was turned so that he rested his chin on its back. He was intently looked down at the un-zipped fly of the man in front of him who was holding his penis for inspection. Sitting next to the Corpsman at the small table were a doctor and a clerk with pencil and paper.

"Peel it back", the Corpsman ordered the man in front of him.

"Now skin it forward."

"Skin it hard and force it forward," he told the man who did not take the inspection seriously.

"Next", he said after each examination.

"Next, next," and the lines of green clad men inched forward toward the inspection tables where they gave their names, unzipped their pants and exposed their penis.

This was a big change of duty for Corpsman who a few months ago were being called to tend the wounded.

We had been in China only a few weeks and the cases of venereal disease had increased dramatically following the reclusive duty of Guam. On Guam only a few men dared to venture into the native villages to meet women. Here with hun-dreds of thousands of women ready to sell their bodies for a few cents, female contact was easy.

"Johnson, skin it back, skin it forward. Good next."

"Garcia, skin her back. Good. Next."

"Jones, ok".

"Do that again Jones, Skin her hard coming forward."

Jones had a little moisture coming out of his penis the first time he skinned it forward. On the second try his penis dripped with a few drops of puss-like substance.

"Stand over there Jones. Next."

Jones was now in line to see the doctor who would take a closer look at the suspicious penis, ask some questions and perhaps prescribe something or have the man report for further examination in the morning.

The long, green lines of men joking, smoking, and swearing at the cold wind that chilled them, swore at the doctors and the Corpsmen who called them out on such a cold day. They swore at the prostitutes who, "probably gave me a dose of clap", too.

Argyrol was prescribed for infections of various kinds including those of the urethra. Its deep purple hue was familiar to all of us in the Pacific. Its value was probably marginal, and the introduction of penicillin at that time had rescued many of us from the consequences of venereal and other diseases as well.

The training films and the lectures about venereal disease were repeated frequently with orders to use condoms or "rubbers" as we called them. Condoms were issued by the Corpsmen if requested.

If you bought condoms from the local Chinese pharmacy usually operated by a Caucasian person you got outdated German supplies of the product. The store-bought condoms would often come apart when applied, or during intercourse, leading to the embarrassment of the Marines as they were jeered by the Chinese prostitutes.

◆   ◆   ◆

China was a constantly changing experience compared to the boredom of Guam. We were in a large, extremely poor country in a civil war. Most of the land mass was controlled by the Communists, while the Nationalist held on to a narrow area along the coast which included Tsingtao. I never thought I would be affected by this war otherwise, I would have been more concerned.

We were involved mostly as a deterrent presence for the Communists. We would go on long marches into the mountains just to show we were there. From where we camped we could hear the artillery duels between the Mao and Chiang armies. Occasionally in the mountains we would encounter small units of the Nationalist army who were our allies during the war and we were surprised how badly dressed they were. They wore old, bulky, quilted uniforms that fit poorly.

The economy was very shaky and inflation was ridiculous. A bottle of Tsing-tao beer cost about twenty-five thousand Chinese dollars, a prostitute charged the same amount in the streets, and a steak and egg lunch cost twice that amount. Twenty five thousand dollars equaled twenty five American cents. The currency fluctuated from day to day and often hourly. One American dollar would at times be worth one hundred thousand Chinese and more.

Throughout the city men and women standing on street corners would shout to Marines, "Change money? Change money, Joe?", holding out huge wads of Chinese paper money in their hands. They were anxious to get American dollars for Chinese Yuan. In the interchange they made a small profit that was important for their livelihood. It was a joke to us who would have to carry twenty five thousand dollar bills in Chinese money when we went on liberty, otherwise you could not fit the smaller denominations in your pockets.

As ubiquitous as the money changers in the streets, were the young boys who were pimping for their mothers, sisters and girl friends. "Nice, crean girl, Joe? Velly crean." they would offer passers by.

"How much?,"

"One dolla, Joe, one dolla. Velly crean, my sister."

The idea of pimping for a sister or mother was very disturbing to understand until you got a glimpse of the wicked poverty that shackled them.

Families consisting of father, mother, and grandparents, and children all lived in a large, box like hut perhaps less than ten foot square, made of discarded pieces of wood and cardboard. A small charcoal stove was kept barley glowing to keep away death from the cold, and to save on the fuel. Thousands of these box homes were in the wretched parts of the city. From these boxes emerged the young prostitute and their pimp brothers hoping to make enough to keep the family alive for another day.

When I saw to one of these boxes that served as homes I was very disturbed that people lived that way. Old parents or grandparents, ill and hungry, dying under layers of dirty rags, looked up at you like sick animals. There was no water to wash and no light except for the charcoal glow and maybe a candle. The toilet would be anywhere outside the box and the place stunk of urine and feces. Adding to the ominous environment was the periodic rumble of artillery in the mountains reminding them of possible future danger.

Mao and his armies were waiting to come in when the Marines left. I found no romance in this aspect of my China experience and felt deep sorrow for the millions of poor Chinese souls. If I were in their place perhaps the words of the

Communist Mao would also sound appealing. The majority of these people had reached the bottom rung of existence.

Most of the Marines in the Tsingtao went to the downtown area for when they left the base on liberty. In the business section one could find modern shops, many clubs catering to the military and civilians, restaurants and of course, bordellos. Few went to the residential sections of the city to explore. Actually there was little to explore in the residential areas unless you were a student of architecture, or just liked to stroll the quiet streets and see how more affluent Chinese lived. As in all cities of the world, there were the wealthy sections and the poor. I had met the poor and wanted to meet those who were better off, and would in time.

Tsingtao had more bordellos than customers to use them. Large multi-storied buildings were used as bordellos. They were three or four stories high with a central courtyard and a main, usually gated, entrance through which you had to pass to enter. There were probably back doors, but they were for the residents. The occupants of the building were workers, soldiers, families with children, and the prostitutes. They all lived together.

Young prostitutes would line up in a row for inspection by the prospective customers on command of their employer. They were all young and of various physical charm. Those who were more attractive knew their status and remained aloof of the gazes of the Marines who viewed the offerings of the day. Some wore transparent clothing and were very forward, touching the men at the crotch to induce an erection and then exclaiming with feigned horror, "Aye too big You too big for me." The Marine would feel flattered and blush.

There was always the smell of cooking rice and vegetables, mingled with the odor of bad plumbing. Conversations of mundane matters, giggles of the girls, and the stern look of the 'Mama' when they got too boisterous created a "homey" atmosphere.

Groups of Marines and sailors would gather to view the girls who lined up before them. When one fell under the charm of a particular young lady he would indicate his choice. It was not unlike a slave market. The Mama would quickly enter a large room which could be divided into cubicles by curtaining a section for the young lovers. Wires at the ceiling permitted the curtains, usually soiled, to be drawn and retracted as necessary for modesty sake. Couples would be in their embraces, separated from each other only by a thin curtain, often only a bed sheet.

It was not an atmosphere conducive for romance but Marines were young, unsophisticated and boiling with teen age testosterone. There was no type of sexual activity that could not be bought here for a price.

A smaller prostitution activity was run by Europeans who employed European and Eurasian women, and other variations of nationalities. These women became very popular when the demand for Chinese prostitutes waned, and word of mouth endorsements by previous customers reached the troops. They were usually located in rooms above a bar or restaurant and did not have the complement of women that the Chinese had.

The men would buy over-priced, and often watered, drinks at the bar and line up along the stairs leading to the rooms above. The entire length of the stair was occupied on a typical night by waiting customers, Marines and sailors, holding drinks and smoking cigarettes chatting or waiting in silence as the line inched forward to the top. At the top of the stairs there was a dimly lit hall with a small card table at one end where an older woman sat with a stack of numbered cards and a box full of money.

As a man came out of one of the rooms he approached the table and returned a numbered card to the woman who placed it at the bottom of the stack. There were perhaps five or six rooms in business each night.

The woman would then call the next man in line to her table and give him a card from the top and collect the fee. Sometimes a house would have a particular star prostitute who could demand a higher fee. This would lead into negotiations between the customer and the lady in charge. Otherwise the fee at that time was about four or five dollars. The Chinese girls in the large houses were possibly getting two dollars depending how business was for the night. Inflation had driven the price of prostitution up from our first days in China when twenty five cents, and less, was all that was asked.

The man with the top card number would go to his room and usually take pot luck as to whom he would share the next few minutes. Some of the regular customers knew some of the girls by a name and would possibly ask for a particular person, but most times it was pot luck.

The rotation of the room numbers gave each prostitute a little time to freshen up between engagements, but time was money and not wasted.

When the customer entered the room he found a large bed, chair and bits of furniture and perhaps a picture on the wall. There were curtains on the windows and the room appeared reasonably clean. It was a far cry from the curtain partitioned working area of the Chinese girls. On the bed would be the prostitute, still moist from her last encounter, wearing a sheer garment and on the floor next to the bed a large pot of water and basin.

The woman would leave it up to customer how much of his clothing he would remove before beginning the romance. As he entered she set a large clock at her night table and it would begin clicking away his time. He had ten minutes and after ten he ran into overtime and added charges, which was rare. Considering the ticking clock, many just un-zipped and were ready for love.

Most of the young men finished before their allotted time and left the room as the woman squatted over the basin and gave herself a perfunctory douche and was ready for the next customer. Some men kept their eye on the ticking clock attempting to delay their ejaculation, but this was a losing game. The professional began to rotate her hips and perform other maneuvers that brought the young man to paradise very quickly. 'Le petite morte', in French.

Some of these women had photos of their families displayed about the room which they rented as living quarters for themselves. Faces of husbands and children peered down at the customers as they collect their four or five dollars worth of pleasure from her flesh. I wondered how life's circumstances brought them to this place. I knew that poverty often explained the Chinese prostitute's choice, of labor, but these women had more complicated problems.

As you left the bar and entered the street you were surrounded by a bunch of beggar children beseeching, "Cumsaw, cumsaw, no mamma, no papa," holding out dirty hands for some sort of contribution. Crippled children, dirty children, malformed children, starving children, China had them by the millions, and they filled the streets begging.

The streets, in good weather, would be full of people at various activities, venders selling food, rickshaw men yelling at each other for right of way; the smell, sound and sight of China would overwhelm you. The smell of this city in this area was that of boiling rice and vegetables and open canals containing human waste.

The 'cumshaw' beggars circled you until rewarded with a coin or cigarette. I saw one approach a British petty officer and realized his error, pulled back saying, "He got no money."

The Americans had money and were the prime benefactors of beggars. The world had changed, and the British who once were the rulers of the waves, had been reduced in status, even in the eyes of street beggars.

◆   ◆   ◆

I "failed" to salute a group of officers one day, and was ordered to explain the oversight to the executive officer. He was an Annapolis graduate and USMC, no R. That made him a regular Marine, not a reserve as most of us were. All spit and polish, close cropped hair, a poster Marine. He had never been in combat.

"Don't you like the Marines, Private?"

I gave him the answer he did not want to hear.

"No sir," I said. The 'Sir' always stuck in my throat.

The Corps knew how to handle insubordinates. They thought they did any way. My authority complex was no mystery to them, and what better way to break that complex than to assign me not only to KP, but KP in the officer's mess, as a waiter. This was very sever punishment for one who had difficulty with authority.

Many of the officers were a few years older than I. Of course, they all had college backgrounds and came from a civilian life much more elite than mine. I resented them that, but I envied their status and planned to attain it some day myself, but for now, they were the enemy.

It was breakfast mess for the officers and I reported for duty. There they were, all the handsome, young, educated officers chatting about things I never heard about. So confident and assured with their position in the Corps having assholes like me do the dirty work. The place settings were clean and orderly with utensils and china rather than the aluminum mess gear of the enlisted mess. I was in agony in this surrounding.

There had to be a way out of this situation.

As I was carrying a plate of scrambled eggs to my first table. I got this vision of the eggs falling from the plate with the home fries onto a second lieutenant's head and dripping down on to his clean, starched khaki shirt. My vision became reality and I was ushered out of the mess hall and chewed out.

The young officer who was the victim of my planned clumsiness suspected it was intentional but never made an issue of it. Rather than keep such a menace in the officers mess and suffer the possibility of more disasters, they demoted me to the enlisted man's mess where I belonged. They put me in charge of the garbage detail.

Being in charge of garbage cans which needed emptying several times during a meal put me a position of unexpected power. The local Chinese knew when the

Marines ate and when they were ready to empty their garbage. Many were starving to death here and access to garbage for sustenance was very important.

China was very backward, and the people continued ancient customs that the Communists promised to change. Rickshaws were still in use, you still saw many women with deformed bound feet on which they could not walk. Young girls were still sold as servants or prostitutes, and in the urban areas, killed at birth.

In the city you could see many people at night preparing to sleep in store fronts and alleyways wrapping themselves with cardboard and paper. Often you could see sick people defecating in the open. Many who were ill, died on the sidewalks and streets and had to be removed every day.

Knowing this, you could understand why a handful of garbage to eat could be so important.

As the Marines filed out of the mess hall, a crowd of Chinese men, women, and children would line up along the fence that separated them from the Marine mess. They carried empty cans in their hands which they extended for food. They were begging for some of the garbage that the Marines were emptying into a large garage can. The garbage container would be loaded with remains of coffee, various drinks, pieces of food, bread, vegetables, pieces of meat and other leftovers, all swimming together in a swirl of garbage.

Many of these people did not have a handful of rice to eat all day. The sight and the odor of the garbage was like an ambrosia to them as it would be to any human who had gone without food for a long period. With expressionless faces they stood there with their pathetic clothing hanging on emaciated bodies, reaching out their empty cans towards me and the garbage can.

Someone had ordered the Chinese away from the fence but they returned for every meal. It embarrassed most of us to see humans begging for garbage, but some Marines forgot that they were human and saw them as just a "bunch of gooks" looking for a "handout".

Dispersing them was like trying to chase a flock of sparrows away from the droppings of a horse in the street. When startled they would disperse in a flurry of movement only to return as soon as no one was there to chase them. In the end they would win out and remain at the fence, begging until the meal was over.

At the end of the meal only a few Chinese workers on my garbage detail remained on duty, and they were not compassionate with their fellow Chinese. I noticed, standing at the fence, one young kid not much younger than I, who had a sad and sullen look on his face. Clearly hungry, but too proud to hold out his can and beg for food, he just stood there waiting. I admired that. I got an urge to make the kid a big Spam sandwich from the mess.

I called the young kid through the gates and offered him the sandwich which he quickly put under his shirt to hide it from the others. Then he pointed to the garbage can and indicated he wanted to dip his tin can into it, too. The thick sandwich was just a moment's bit of good luck for him but the garbage can would be part of his continuing life.

How many Spam sandwiches could I make to feed the people outside those gates? How many sandwiches would it take to feed the starving people of China tonight and every night of their lives? I knew I could not work out a solution. The world had to work out a way to provide Spam sandwiches for all the starving people holding empty cans outside barbed wire fences. I felt no sense of superiority. I knew from the war how quickly hunger could reduce arrogance to humility.

◆　　　◆　　　◆

During our tour in China some of us adopted needy, young Chinese boys around the city as mascots. These kids would run errands and spend their days around the Marines learning English in its most colorful expressions, and doing various errands from shining shoes to washing clothing. Very soon they became familiar with various aspects of Marine life. They were paid a few dollars and given cut down Marine uniforms to wear. After a time these kids became very attached to their Marine friends and felt they were actually part of the Corps.

One of these boys was a personable little teenager who was small for his age due to malnutrition. He was called Charlie Two Shoes, (Tu Shu, his name) and fitted with several cut down uniforms that replicated the real thing. His photo was printed in the local and Marine papers, and he became a minor celebrity. When the Marines left China they left Charlie Two Shoes in Tsingtao, but used all their influence to have him come to the States before the Communist took over.

When Charlie Two Shoes came to America he opened a Chinese Restaurant, got married and had a family. His life had turned from Chinese street urchin to American businessman. Through the years some American news papers would periodically feature the story of Charlie Two Shoes and his friends, the Marines.

But he was only one of millions of young kids who got a chance. The rest had to face their future in a China going through a painful transition.

◆   ◆   ◆

I left on liberty one afternoon and passed through the main gate of the University where the Marine guards checked out the liberty passes. I pushed through the hoard of rickshaw men who gathered to pick up fares just as taxi drivers did at airports. It was the same every day at the liberty hour, the pushing and shoving of the rickshaw men, and the Marines filing out in clean uniforms, well fed, the product of a world power. The rickshaw men were the product of a corrupt government that was soon to taste Communism and its own brand of exploitation and pain. Not many Marines gave that any thought on their way to the dance bars.

How quickly one becomes acclimated to inhumanity. At first I would not ride in a rickshaw for humanitarian reasons and then slowly I rationalized, I could not change it. I compensated for this rationalization by always giving the rickshaw man a large tip and always walking up the steep inclines rather than have him pull me. The Chinese civilians, and most Marines I saw, seldom dismounted on steep climbs, and sat as the rickshaw man struggled upward.

If the rickshaw men were not jostling for fares to the city, they squatted on their haunches, smoking cigarettes held between their thumb and index finger in the Asian fashion. The butts were so small that they burned their finger tips but they held them gingerly, shifting their hold as they sucked in the smoke in contentment. The local tobacco was dark, strong and mixed with other foreign material that burned with a strong, black smoke. A slight wince would crease their faces, and their eyes would squint as they drew in the smoke and felt its satisfying burn.

When they could hold the small butt no more, they would carefully extinguish it and place the unused tobacco in a container with other butts. When ready, the man would collect the tobacco from these butts into a pipe and smoke it down to nothing. Every rickshaw man carried one of these small, bronze bowled, long stemmed, pipes for this purpose. The nicotine and tar of many smokes stained the pipe bowls, and the fingers, lips and teeth of the smokers. Rickshaw boys had brown and black teeth, and they were never fat.

Their skin, over lean muscle, especially those of the legs, often pressed on bones and ligaments that protruded as they ran along the streets. Their heads were usually shaved and they wore little clothing, even in winter. Most wore scarps of clothing, ill fitting shirt and pantaloons. Their shoes were either straw soled, or made from a piece of an old auto tire.

Rickshaws were owned by an organization or person who rented it to the man who pulled it. Although his perspiration and the rubbing of his palms had stained the rickshaw poles that he pulled all year long, the vehicle belonged to someone else who was very strict about its use and condition. Quite often a drunken sailor or Marine would abuse a rickshaw man and kick his rickshaw wheels out of shape because of a fare dispute. It shamed me when this happened but there was no way to solve the injustice and one had to become calloused to it.

The rickshaw man cried as he tried to repair the damage that took money needed to feed his family. The young Marines and sailors, often drunk, would never know the tragedy they had caused by his bullying tantrum. The Americans, I felt, always had a superiority attitude toward the Asians whether they were Japanese enemies, or Chinese allies. The only reason for this attitude that I could see was that we were powerful and rich, and they were defeated and poor.

I was very impressed by rickshaw men who did this denigrating work of transporting fellow humans. They had to have tremendous stamina. As they pulled their fares along the streets throughout the day they learned how to conserve their energy. On shallow downward slopes they would allow the wheels to lift the poles and raise them in the air so that they glided along with the passenger with feet off the ground. They had to balance the vehicle precisely to keep themselves in the air. A good rickshaw man was able to do this many times during a ride and rest his weary legs.

"Here Joe, here, me number one Lickshaw." They shouted to the Marines who were looking for transportation into the city.

They were the only public transportation available. Often the competition for fares would lead to pushing fights and shouts of contempt, but never did they try to damage the other man's rickshaw.

As the Marines chose their rickshaw man they shouted the destination they wanted. When people don't speak the language they tend to shout louder to be understood. If the rickshaw man knew the place he was supposed to go it was not a problem, but if not, the passenger had to give directions all the way. Most fares were headed for the central part of the city where the girls and bars would be.

I had learned a little Chinese from the men who worked in my garbage detail and was able to use many common expressions in conversation. I was able to tell my rickshaw man my destination without shouting or loud explanations.

"Kinkow ee Loo", (Kinkow First Road), I said.

The rickshaw man nodded, understanding. Then realizing that I was an American and speaking Chinese he looked over his shoulder and smiled.

"Sheh Sheh," he said. (Thank you.)

The rickshaw rolled smoothly down the long, sloping road that led from the main gate to a residential area of affluent homes. It was a short and easy rickshaw ride that gave me little guilt. The large homes were protected by eight foot brick walls that were about two feet thick and had broken glass bottles imbedded into the cement at the top to discourage trespassers.

I got off at the bottom of Kinkow First Road and paid the rickshaw man his asking fee without complaint, plus a generous tip, to salve my conscience anyway. The man was grateful for not having to climb the steep incline that the road made to the top. He was also happy that he had overcharged me in the fare before receiving his generous tip. I did not care because it was all part of the adventure for me.

I asked him for a light for my cigarette, "Nee yu yan whah ma?", and he lit a match.

Smoking my cigarette, carrying my silver headed cane for protection, I climbed the hill in the brisk autumn weather. It was so good to be young and alive with a little money in my pocket in a strange and exciting land. The days of Okinawa were fading into the past very quickly

On subsequent rides to Kinkow Road, I would ask the rickshaw man to change places with me and I would be the driver and he the passenger. I wanted to experience the feeling. After protesting, but convinced by the money I offered him, the man would agree. He took the passenger seat and I fitted myself between the two pulling poles and began to trot away to his delight. I did not run for a long time, but did get the feel of it.

As I walked up Kinkow Road I noticed that it was an upper class neighborhood. The homes were all large and multi-level, constructed of stone and brick and situated on a large plot of land. All the homes had the high concrete and stone wall surrounding them with the embedded broken glass on the top. Some had barbed wire in addition to the embedded glass. It was a quiet, clean suburban area that had to protect itself from the poverty that surrounded it.

Near the top of Kinkow Road on the right side there was a large property surrounded by a stone wall with a large gate. The gate was open so that I could see a tiny wooden house to the left of the larger, main house. A hand printed, cardboard sign that read, "HOME COOKED MEALS" was nailed to the small house.

Sounds good, I thought, and decided to investigate.

To me this was a refreshing prospect after the offerings in the business district where you never knew the quality or cleanliness of the food.

I walked through the gate and knocked at the front door of the cottage where a small, thin man responded. He was bald and had the impish, wrinkled face of a leprechaun. He was smoking a butt of a cigarette and squinted through the smoke that encircled him.

"Hello", he said. "come in" with an accent, and showing two rows of imperfect, yellow teeth that had not seen a dentist for many years.

A large, brown German police dog stood behind him and quietly appraised me as I entered, and emitted a low growl of disapproval that was barely discernable, emanating from deep inside his chest. Nevertheless, I heard it and was on guard. The little man made a very subtle movement with his hand that I could not describe and the dog ceased his intimidation. The room was heated by a small pot belly stove that glowed where the coal had collected and gave off a low, comforting hiss. A young Chinese servant did kitchen work behind the little man although they had no customers.

"I'm Paul Skorniakoff," he said with an air of pride as though announcing something very important, and then added, "You can call me Pop.

I did not know that this meeting was the beginning of a friendship that would last as long as we lived.

The fifty five year old man, and I, were thirty five years apart in age but he had something about him that made us fast friends. I liked him immediately,

"Take off your coat and sit down," he said, "would you like something to eat?"

I said, "Yes, what do you have?"

"Steak and eggs all right?", he asked, knowing this was the favorite food of the Americans in China.

"Sounds good," I said, and immediately Pop gave the order in Chinese to his young Chinese helper in the kitchen.

In a few minutes the sizzle and smell of frying meat, eggs and potatoes filled the little cottage and the dog began licking his chops with a huge, red tongue that slapped against his jaws. Then in his impatience he whined, fidgeted and yawned, revealing long, white, pointed, intimidating, and surprising clean teeth.

Pop, annoyed with the dog's behavior, whispered something in Russian, and the dog changed his location in the room, placed his muzzle on his paws, and pretended to sleep.

The bungalow consisted of four rooms, a small cooking area behind a kitchen, two closet-like bedrooms and a combination sitting/dining room where he served his friends and guests. The small building looked fragile and vulnerable to all the elements. It was built only a few yards away from the main house which was very substantially built with stone and bricks. The larger, two story house was owned by a Chinese family, Pop later told me, comprised of a father and daughter team of lawyers. The daughter had two children who were in grade school. The Skorniakoffs rented the small house from them.

Pop lived with his wife and daughter who on that day were working in the city for the Red Cross as secretaries and translators. Both mother and daughter, spoke several languages and were skilled in office procedures. They had quickly applied for employment when the Americans entered the area.

The war had been over only a few months and the Communist army of General Mao was encircling the Tsingtao area. Scattered remnants of the defeated Japanese army were ready to formally surrender to the Marines who were there to accept. The Japanese would then be transported to Japan.

The Skorniakoffs were among several thousand White Russians (White in opposition to Red for political distinction) who found refuge in China following the Russian Revolution in 1917. These people had lived in various Chinese cities including Peking, Tiensin and Tsingtao in North China. As Russian expatriates they formed communities that were able to survive with most of their culture in tact. Their religion, food, holidays and language were all maintained in the close community. They even had a cultural center in Peking during the early days where they would produce plays, and concerts by Russian and Chinese artists. Pop's talent as a puppeteer and doll maker sustained the family. He was noted for his puppet shows which were popular in the Russian community.

Pop had been a captain in the Russian Army and had escaped the Communist after the revolution by making his way to China across Mongolia, by train, foot and whatever transportation available. When he reached Peking, he joined the exiled community of Russians and soon found a wife. She was the daughter of a Russian man who was an engineer for a gold mine on a small island off the coast of China near Vladivostok. Stranded by the revolution the family made its home in North China, The daughter was married to a man who deserted her, leaving her to provide for a daughter by herself, after her parents died.

Now in 1945, after almost thirty years in China, they found themselves in Marine occupied North China as expatriates of Communist Russia. The war was over, but they could not return to Russia for political reasons. The Americans were their temporary protectors from the Chinese Communists who would soon take the entire country. They found themselves with no place to go, as did hundred of thousands of others after the war, all labeled as displaced persons.

Their years in China had not been luxurious, but they did manage with the help of the community to enjoy as much as they could. Always a suspicious minority in a foreign land, they did their best to learn the language and customs and still retain their own identity. Considering the standard of living in China during the decades of the twenties, and thirties, life had not been easy.

◆　　　◆　　　◆

The young servant who Skorniakoff called Wen, was done with the steak, eggs and potatoes and placed them on the table. Wen was dressed in black which was a sort of uniform of the day at that time for students and working class people. He was about my age perhaps a few years older, twenty two or so and had a nice clean cut look about him and bowed when he served the plate and looked at Pop for further instructions which Pop gave in Chinese, very professionally, without sign of familiarity. He was the boss talking to his servant. I knew Pop was not a rich man by the way he was living in this small, rented house. He could afford a servant only because of the poverty of China.

I got up from my chair to go to the table where Wen had set my food, and the dog showed that he was aware of my movement by emitting a noise from his belly.

"Russo" Pop said the dog's name in Russian. He then winked at me and said, "Eat, we will entertain you."

As I sat at the dinner table Pop put a morsel of food on the tip of Russo's nose and said something to him in Russian. The dog remained absolutely still with his eyes crossed, looking at the food at the tip of his long snout. But he did not move to take it. He was a large dog with black and brown running through him and his eyes had that silver spark with tinges of gold that flicked on and off.

Pop and I continued to talk about where I came from and my family and all the while he smiled at me and indicated his glee by motioning toward Russo who was frustrated, but obedient, during the oft repeated act he was being put through. After quite a while I felt sorry for Russo and told Pop to let him have the meager tidbit. Pop said, "No, a little longer"

I continued with my meal, and Russo, despite the pressure he was under, emitted a warning growl at me if I made a move he did not like. I felt sorry for the poor beast anyway, and admired his obedience.

After several minutes Pop gave Russo a signal I could not detect and Russo snapped the food off his nose and into his mouth in one smooth movement that produced a sharp clap of his jaws. He licked out his long tongue and showed his impressive and intimidating teeth again in a big yawn. Then he returned to his crouching position by the fire. He had worked very hard for a bit of food. His eyes alternately open and closed. When open, you could not read his mood, and when closed, you dared not assume he was asleep.

I fully understood what Pop meant when he said, "He's a good dog, he won't bite you,—unless I tell him to."

In a way I was impressed by Russo's patience and obedience to his master, but then too, even though he was a dog, I pitied him his lack of pride and independence, his complete surrender to authority.

◆   ◆   ◆

The day passed but I returned several more times for "home cooked meals" and some conversation with Pop. I had been introduced to his family only through his stories and the photos of the two woman that were displayed on the shelves. During each visit I got to know them better through Pop's stories, and soon I would meet them.

I had come into Pop's house one dusty, windy autumn afternoon hungry as hell and annoyed with the weather.

"What's all that dust blowing around the city?", I asked.

Pop continued reading his paper and he casually said, "Gobi."

That mysterious and romantic word suddenly reminded me where I was. My days had been occupied with mundane chores of Marine duty and I took my geography for granted. I could just as well had been in Hackensack, New Jersey on some of those days. But now I heard the word Gobi and realized it was the desert sands blowing out of Mongolia, the home of Genghis Khan, the Dahli Llama, etc. etc.

The word Gobi became personally familiar to me now that I was inhaling its dust and grit. It joined the other words I recently made personal, like Guadalcanal, Guam, Ulithi, Okinawa, Saipan, Tinian, Kinugawa Maru, Coral Sea, North China Sea, Sea of Japan.

Gobi dust from Tibet was part of our conversation just like discussing the rain in Florida or the snow in New Hampshire. It made me feel world traveled and sophisticated. None of my friends back home had ever breathed dust from the Gobi. Pop Skorniakoff had seen Gobi dust blow across the land for nearly thirty years and the excitement and romance of it, if there ever was any, was gone.

Many Chinese wore a gauze mask when Gobi dust was in the air of North China. I was amazed that dust could be blown for such great distances without dissipating. Here we were on the coast of eastern China in the seaport city of

Tsingtao being powdered by Gobi dust. It was so romantic to me, I forgot the irritation.

◆   ◆   ◆

During one visit to Pop's cottage on Kinkow Road I mentioned my interest in learning to speak Chinese.

"I would like to study some Chinese while I am in China," I told Pop, "Do you know where I could take lessons?"

"Madam Do, my land lady, may be interested in teaching you," he said.

"Do you think she would take me as a student?", I asked.

"I think so, I'll ask her and let you know."

That day Pop had some friends over as guests who sat around smoking and drinking hot tea from large glasses. They would pop a cubes sugar or hard candy in their mouths and then slurp in hot tea with a hissing sound to cool it before they swallowed. They jovially spoke in several languages. In the small gatherings some spoke Russian, others in French, and English, of course. Chinese was just used when they spoke to Wen. The men and women sat together around the little sitting room, and I observed with great interest as much as I could. Pop knew I enjoyed being there, and translated the conversations for me when necessary.

These older people had experienced much more life than I had and they were sophisticated about politics and world events way beyond my ability to understand. Their familiarity with several languages impressed me and I intended to add Chinese to my language ability although my English at that time could stand improvement too.

I met Pop's wife Antonia Skorniakoff during this visit and liked her immediately. She was a very attractive woman, taller than Pop, and had this perpetual smile on her lips as though ready to share a joke with you. She insisted on changing my name from Lance to Lania, more suitable for a Russian society, and I was ordered to call her, "Mom."

The Skorniakoff's daughter, Julia, was a shy girl about my age and very serious. She spoke several languages including English, like her mother, and played the piano with some accomplishment. Whenever we were in the same company she tended to allow her parents to do the talking and made comments in Russian thus excluding me. I took no offense to this, but my friendship was more with the parents.

Before I left that wonderful party, Pop told me "Lania, I spoke with Madam Do and she would like to meet you to discuss your Chinese lessons."

He gave me the date I was expected to come to meet her.

◆   ◆   ◆

It was during Christmas week of 1945 that I saw Pop again. I wanted to show my appreciation for the meals he made for me (and never took payment) and the contact with Madam Do. He had mentioned that he had not had a fresh lemon in years and he enjoyed lemon with his tea. Also he loved to smoke American cigarettes, especially the strong, dark tobacco in Camels, and he enjoyed American beer.

I put a plan together that would make a merry holiday for the Skorniakoffs. My easy access to mess supplies made the requisition of fresh lemons a simple matter. There were always a case or two of beer around the barracks either for sale or ready for requisitioning. To my mind the beer was superfluous. After drinking the locally brewed Tsingtao beer I would not drink American beer in China, but perhaps Pop had become too accustomed to the local brew and had a taste for the American brew.

Obtaining Camel cigarettes was no problem either, and I bought a few cartons for little money. Now I had all the holiday gifts I needed to surprise the Skorinakoffs.

The remaining problems were, transportation to Kinkow First Road, (I could not transport this stuff by rickshaw.) and a pass to go through the Shantung University gates with my gifts.

LaFoo had connections in the motor pool and would be able to get me a jeep for a few hours without difficulty that was relatively easy. But who would drive it? Who else but LaFoo. The authority to pass through the gates was another thing.

I had among my possessions at that time a pair of small gold stars that I had bought in one of the Chinese markets because they were a bargain and looked pretty. If I placed those stars on the shoulders of my overcoat, from a distance a guard at the gate would think they were some kind of officer emblem shining in the sun and be ready to salute. He would not ask for a pass.

LaFoo agreed to my plan. We had done more risky things than this in our time, and he helped me load the jeep with lemons, cigarettes and beer. I put the stars on my shoulders, put on a pair of sun glasses and tried to look big and important sitting next to my driver.

I told LaFoo to drive to the north gate which was used for vehicles.

"Just slow down a little as we near the guard, and when he raises his rifle to give a salute, just shoot pass him."

When I returned the salute I tried to obscure my face and the emblem on my shoulder in a sloppy hand and arm motion. The guard could see the glint of the emblem but not the actual design. If he saw the stars I would be done. But stars were all the I had, I had no bars.

LaFoo loved the whole thing and obeyed my suggestions exactly and off we went toward Kinkow Road which was less than ten minutes away by jeep.

The exhaust from the jeep escaped in a thin white wisp of smoke that seemed to freeze in the air as we reached the Kinkow Road hill and passed the walled mansions with the embedded broken glass on the wall tops. Behind us was Tsingtao harbor loaded with ships from all over the world and the American Navy keeping law and order. In a few minutes we were turning into Pop's driveway.

Pop, hearing the jeep enter the front yard, was at the door squinting to see who was coming to see him.

"Lania," he cried out when he saw me. "What are you doing with a jeep?"

When he spotted the two stars I had forgotten to remove from my shoulder during the ride to his house, he slapped the side of his cheek and said mockingly, "You are a General now, Lania?"

I realized my mistake and quickly removed the emblems. I did not want to explain that part to him.

He stepped aside the door to allow me and LaFoo to carry the gifts into the house and then he followed us with his eyes full of questions. He saw the beer immediately and was pleased. When he saw the Camels cigarette cartons come out of the bag he was in awe.

I introduced him to LaFoo who he hugged and kissed on both cheeks. LaFoo, although part French, winced.

Then I grabbed the bag of big, yellow, juicy lemons and spilled them over the table top allowing them to roll in an avalanche unto the floor and Pop scrambled to catch them. He grabbed one of the yellow fruit and with a paring knife cut the end off it and popped it into his mouth, skin and all.

Had tears in his eyes, and a look of joy filled his face. I realized how such a small thing could bring happiness. It was so genuine a pleasure for a simple thing.

"Oh, Lania," he said. "Oh my dear boy, Lania. Oh my dearest friend, Lania."

And then he reached an arm around my neck and pulled me to him to kiss my cheeks. I could smell the strong fragrance of lemon on his breath as he turned from one cheek to the other. He then did the same to LaFoo who resisted a little.

LaFoo and I were anxious to return the jeep to the motor pool, so we left Pop among his lemons with moist eyes. I told him that I would see him later in the day when I had official liberty so that I could meet Madam Do to discuss Chinese lessons.

The whole escapade had taken us little more than a half hour and I returned sitting in the jeep as a Private. I never used the stars again.

When I returned later in the day Pop was still full of thanks for my gifts, especially the lemons.

"Come," he said, "Madam Do will be waiting for us."

He took my arm and led me out of his cottage.

Madam Do's house was a three story, stone structure that had about fourteen rooms. Several men were working around the property cleaning debris and performing odd jobs as Pop and I approached the front door. Pop rang the doorbell and smiled at me.

"She's expecting us around this time," he said.

A young girl servant came to the door and spoke to Pop in Chinese and we were led to the interior of the house through a large center hall, and into a large sitting room where we were asked to sit down.

"Cheeng dsaw," the girl said, please sit.

"Sheh sheh," Pop said. I already knew that this meant thanks.

We could hear children laughing and playing in some distant room.

In a few minutes a small woman with a light complexion and a pretty smile showing extremely white teeth came into the room. We both stood up to greet her.

"Ah, Madam Do," Pop said with a genuine pleasure, and then they spoke in Russian which Pop translated to me as we went along.

I noticed that the Europeans did not speak to educated Chinese in their language if they both knew a Western language. I assumed that the European did not have the proficiency in speaking Chinese as the Chinese had in the Western language. I knew that Madam Do did not speak English, but she spoke Russian, Japanese and French.

"Lania," Pop said, "Madam Do says she is happy to meet you and will gladly teach you Chinese."

I thanked her and said I, too, was glad to meet her.

Pop translated this into Russian.

Madam Do wore a black smock that fit her loosely. It had a high, Chinese style, collar with a little yellow design around it. She was about five foot three and had a slim body. She wore no makeup and her skin was clear and healthy. Her jet black hair was cut a mannish style which she parted on the left and combed on side of her head. She conveyed to me a sense of efficiency and honest purpose without extraneous affectations. Her open, honest and captivating smile was reassuring to me as her new student. When she extended her hand she had a firm grip of a business woman who had associated with European men. She then took a step back and bowed a little from her waist in the manner of her own heritage.

I returned her bow the best I could thinking this was the proper etiquette.

Madam Do proposed to teach me Chinese by communicating only in Chinese and referring to a dictionary to teach me words and phrases. I was a high school drop out, and was wanting in my own language, but I had a desire to learn. I put myself in her hands. We agreed to meet twice a week and I promised to do a lot of homework to make more progress. The two, one hour lessons would cost five dollars a week. She soon refused to take the fee.

This tentative agreement was enough to begin and we would improvise as we went along. Madam Do and Pop spoke a little more in Russian and I could see that Pop was joking around because Madam Do was laughing and blushing at the same time. There was this easy, friendly feeling between them that you knew was sincere.

When we had finished Madam Do called her children into the room. She had two boys, about seven and ten years old. They were well mannered and bowed to us and then stood near their mother as we were directed to the exit by the servant girl. My first lesson would begin the next week.

When we were back in the cottage Pop told me that after graduating from Shantung University Madam Do applied for and was accepted to the law school in Harbin University in Manchuria where she graduated as lawyer. Her lawyer father was very happy.

Harbin University law school at that time was an all-male institution and classes were in Russian. Madam Do was the only female and to avoid too much attention she had her hair cut like a man's and wore men's clothing.

Her graduation yearbook, I later saw, carried her photo as one of the graduates. Her cut short, no make up on and wearing the black uniform, she was one of the boys. Harbin at that time in the nineteen twenties was still a gathering place for many Russian political exiles, and it was alive with political and cultural activity that Do Shui Can, her full name, found exciting and interesting. She met her businessman husband in Harbin and later divorced him after one of his business trips to Shanghai, when she learned he had a second wife.

Madam Do then started to practice law with her father in Tsingtao, and took care of her children alone.

◆   ◆   ◆

When I arrived for my first Chinese lesson on Kinkow Road I did not stop to visit Pop, and just went to front door of the big house.

I rang the door bell and a voice asked "Sheh summa?" Who is it?

I answered, "meegwa leeu dyan dwee". American Marine, hoping my pronunciation was understandable.

The door opened and the servant girl smiled at seeing me, knowing that I was due to arrive for my first lesson.

The lesson started with my asking how to say simple sentences and adding words to my vocabulary. I would write the sentences and words on my pad phonetically after asking Madam Do to repeat the pronunciation several times. Some words needed to be pronounced many times before I was able to imitate the sound and some I never got no matter how long she tried to teach me. After the lesson I would return to the barracks at the university and study my notes until my next lesson.

I did not get involved in learning the different tones of the language which is very important, but tried to imitate the sounds that I heard.

The lessons continued this way and I was becoming more proficient by imitating as best I could. However, I never really knew what my progress was because Madam Do was too kind, and always said my Chinese was, "Hun how!" very good, which I doubted.

The only real measure of my learning was by speaking to the local Chinese, and if they understood me, I felt I was learning. I was able to carry on a simple conversation slowly and do some shopping at the local markets. Knowing the language was a great advantage and I'm sure saved me money. The Chinese people I spoke to appreciated my attempt to learn their language no matter how badly I sounded.

During one session Madam Do interrupted the lesson to introduce me to a young girl who she said wanted to learn English. Could she sit in on the lessons with us? I certainly agreed.

"This is Aie Mei Wong," she said and I smiled and said Hello, "Nee how ma?" How are you?

Aie Mai was a slim teenager dressed in the black uniform the students wore with the high Chinese collar and a little embroidery around the fringes. She was tall, about five feet six, had dark, doe like eyes that slanted exotically above a soft, sweet smile. Her black hair was cut just above the shoulders and she wore it parted on the middle and combed back where it was held together on either side with a small clasp. Her skin was clear and smooth without blemish of any kind and her teeth small, even and white. She was a beautiful girl, and I was glad she had joined us.

Our lessons continued for several more sessions but my progress seemed to have slowed because of the time being used to teach English to Aie Mai. I really didn't care because I enjoyed the sessions very much. Madam Do would serve tea and cookies and the hour was extended into an extra half hour before the sessions were done.

Then one evening Madam Do said she had to excuse herself and left Aie Mei and me alone. She did the same on the next night and the next and finally the pattern was set whereby my lessons were mainly with Aie Mei and not Madam Do. It took me a while to understand that she had planned it that way, but I could not understand why. She knew my stay in China was temporary and could end suddenly. To be a match maker for two kids in this situation was inconsiderate of a woman who had a law practice.

Aie Mai and I became friends. Our lessons would develop into short dates where we walked through the streets to window shop, and look at the ships in the harbor. She was very shy and did not make as big an effort to learn English as I did to learn Chinese. We enjoyed each others company. Her mother was a widow and she was an only child. Madam Do was a close family friend. She was in her last year of high school.

As we walked about the streets chatting and laughing, (my Chinese was probably horrible, but she was kind to try understanding it) I would hear comments from the Chinese who passed by or who we passed along the way. I could not make out the meaning of their words but knew that they were not complimentary. Aie Mei would change her expression and I knew she was hurt. The people were calling her names because she was walking with me and probably assumed she was a slut, being with an American. They knew by her bearing and dress that she was an educated girl and not a prostitute.

Realizing the hurt our walks had caused her I suggested that we keep away from the crowds. She denied any hurt but went along with my suggestion, so our walking dates were reduced to areas around the Kinkow Road houses which were quite nice and we got to know some of the neighbors in the area. These people were more educated than the people in the business district and accepted our friendship without insinuations.

I don't know what intricate feelings stirred in me with Aie Mei. I was a teenager too and every pretty girl I met I would have some feeling that could be measured as love. When we were alone in our study room on several occasions we would kiss quickly but always on guard for one of the Do family to come in. We had no opportunity to be intimate even if we wanted that.

Aie Mei would have accepted my advances I'm sure, but I had no intention of becoming too friendly with this young student. If I wanted sex there was a whole city below us full of prostitutes. I wondered if Madam Do had hoped for this too. If I had been irresponsible and fathered a child perhaps that would have bound me to Aie Mei morally, but our friendship was nowhere near that possibility.

I could say we were in love in that strange, youthful time in a world full of danger and pain. But it was not the love of commitment. I felt that I did not want to leave Aie Mei and China that quickly, but that was the nature of my service. More and more units were being shipped back home and the Communist, who Madam Do called, "Hoon Hosas", Red Monkeys, were threatening to come into the city. Soon I would be leaving China.

I felt that Madam Do understood this because one day she invited me to meet her father for dinner. It was a sort of graduation and farewell party although nothing of that kind was mentioned. It was August 1946. I, Aie Mei, Madam Do and her father sat down to an elaborate dinner table that they had prepared in my honor. I was embarrassed because they all spoke Chinese so well and I was a beginner. My attempt to learn their language, however, made me a welcomed friend.

As a house gift I brought Mr. Do, a carton of Lucky Strike Cigarettes and a small book of Chinese poetry which he appreciated very much. Mr. Do was a poet too. He looked like the Mandarin characters in the movies, with long, dropping mustache, and a beard that flowed in long, gray strands from his chin. He was almost six feet tall and wore the black robe with highs collar and long baggy sleeves. When he greeted me he folded is hands over his stomach into the sleeves of the garment he wore and gave a slight bow which I returned. It was obvious that his daughter had spoken to him about me over the past months and he had a good impression of me.

We sat through an awkward dinner together and I was treated to many specialties that I really did not want to taste. There was entire poached fish which Madam Do plucked apart with her chop sticks and offered me the meat around the head. I thought she was going to give me one of the eyes, too, but she didn't. There were steamed buns filled with pork, a lot of vegetables, dumplings, and dishes I did not recognize.

I spoke in my very basic Chinese and Madam Do translated my Chinese to her father who I'm sure did not understand what I said. Ai Mei just lowered her eyes and smiled and said very little. However, we tried to assume a bit of cheer and made the best of the occasion. I realized that the old Mandarin had honored me with this dinner and I gave them many thanks in Chinese when I left. I never saw him again.

◆   ◆   ◆

My lessons and meetings with Aie Mei were interrupted for one week when our regiment went into the nearby hills on maneuvers to remind the Mao army that we were still there. I had no way of contacting my friends since I had no phone and any absence had to be accepted without explanation until we met again, if we did. We never knew after each meeting what the world conditions, and my orders, were would be.

Being on KP did not excuse me from going into the field as an infantryman. The Marines considered every Marine an infantryman first and then a specialist in whatever he was trained in. When men were needed to do grunt work it was assumed that everyone knew how to do it. For that week I returned to infantry duty along with some of my old buddies including LaFoo.

Our maneuvers were very realistic with large convoys of trucks transporting troops, artillery rolling along, accompanied by all the necessary gear for a full field operation. We were never told at our level what it was all about but we assumed it was to show the Communist armies that surrounded us that we were still in charge of this area.

Once our position had been assigned we dug in and assumed that combat conditions were in effect. At times we heard artillery firing in the distant mountains where the Nationalist and Communist armies were engaging. It never occurred to me that we would ever participate in this argument so I was not overly worried. However, when the sound of distant artillery sounded in the distant mountains, it brought back fearful memories of those nightmare nights and days not too far past. Knowing that the sound came from a very long distance away made them tolerable.

During these long, cold days in the mountains we were visited daily by farm women who tried to sell us peanuts for a few Chinese Yuan. Often they were accompanied by their children who enjoyed the Marine company and the candy or other gifts that they would receive. This diversion made the days pass easier especially if one of the peanut women were attractive enough to seduce.

The land was desolate at this time of year and the grass and had tuned brown. Along the roadways you did not see one scrap of paper, a tin can, or piece of wood as you would see in America. Any of this litter was retrieved by the Chinese to be used for some purpose. Paper and wood burned as fuel, a tin can became a cooking utensil or a kitchen tool. The telephone poles were made of concrete because the peasants would cut the wooden poles down in winter for fuel.

A small farmstead was located near our position and you could see several small shacks with thatched roofs and mud packed siding. A anemic spiral of smoke would escape from the small chimneys revealing the frugality of its owners. They had very little fuel to burn to keep warm. The huts were without running water and did not have toilets. If there were animals they were housed in an area separated from the people only by the huts outside wall. No one was fat. No one had radios, No one drank Tsingtao beer here. They wore clothing that was made from a quilt like material that was very bulky but probably quite warm. Men, women, and children were dressed the same.

These peasant lived not too unlike I did before entering the Marines when I lived in a two room apartment without heat with my brother and father. We did not have the luxury of fine food and clothing, but we did have running water and a toilet.

On the last day of our operation we were packing to move back to the Shantung University when one of the peanut woman came around our site selling peanuts from a bag slung around her shoulder. If you bought peanuts she would reach into the bag for the amount that you bought. One or two handfuls or more. She had a small boy with her, probably her son, and we identified her as a young housewife who had visited us before. She was healthy looking with clean smile and skin, not unattractive.

Some of the trucks were already pulling out onto to the roadway leaving our camp site but one Marine approached the peanut woman and suggested with hand gestures that they forget the peanuts and have intercourse. He pointed to the small tent that would be erected quickly for modesty sake and she shyly agreed after sending her little boy off. Realizing that we were about to leave the area forever she probably decided to make a few desperately needed Yuan.

The pup tent went up in seconds and the woman entered, let a front flap of her pantaloons down. One by one the men who were interested entered to make love to the peanut woman. Each had drawn lots to determine position in line. Her son stood in the distance kicking the rocks and sending up little puffs of dust impatient and embarrassed. Was he angry, ashamed, frightened,—aware?

The pup tent came down faster than it went up and our trucks were ready to load our gear. Poverty had conquered the morals of the peanut woman, and lust the morals of the Marines. As the trucks rolled away the peanut woman stood waving in the dust with a few inflated Chinese Yuan in her hand, and the other holding her son.

When the Communist armies eventually came into these mountains when we left, I wondered, would they, too, bargain with the peanut woman?

◆　　　◆　　　◆

I returned to my KP duty and Chinese lessons when we returned to the University. I saw Aie Mei whenever I could to go walking or just to sit and talk in the house or yard. It was a wonderful feeling to be with her and I'm sure she felt the same.

"Whah aie nee" I told her one day, not knowing it would be the last time the I saw her, and she repeated the words in English to me, "I love you."

I would never see her again.

That same summer day in 1946 I went to visit the Skorniakoffs briefly before returning to the barracks and was greeted by Mom and Julia who were in tears.

"They took Pasha away, Lania," Mom said.

"They put him in jail. They won't let us see him."

"What?, why?," I asked.

Then Mom told me that during the Japanese occupation of North China Pop had worked for the Japanese as a guard. It was a simple and temporary job just to put food on the table. Pop, however, was always ashamed of that part of his life and never mention it to anyone. He worked briefly for the Japanese as an unarmed security guard at one of their facilities in Tsingtao. I did not get any more details but automatically assumed Pop had not done anything wrong and was forced into helping the enemy.

The Nationalist now were holding this episode against him and making it a big deal about something they always knew. The Nationalist also knew that Pop was a White Russian, of course, and this placed him between the Nationalist who were soon to lose their control of China. and the Communist who were to take over.

As usual, I overreacted with a display of loyalty that I had learned from the B movies, and took a rickshaw to the jail where Pop was being held and tried to pass through the gates that were guarded by two Nationalist Chinese soldiers. Immediately I was stopped and confronted by the two guards who were holding rifles.

With the arrogance and stupidity of a young Marine I confronted the guards and spoke to them contemptuously with my bad Chinese.

"Whah yow kine e kine wawdeh pungyou," I want to see my friend, I told them. Assuming an air of authority and superiority, I really did not feel, over the Asians.

I liked the Chinese people genuinely.

"Tadeh mienza Skorniakoff," His name is Skorniakoff, I said. And they laughed.

This angered me, and I again assumed a haughty attitude informing them with a pompous demeanor," Whah sheh meegwa jren, boo sheh tsongwa jren." I am an American not Chinese, as though this obvious revelation would startle them.

They got my message and did not like my inference that being American was any more important in the world than being Chinese. They did not laugh anymore and blocked my way with a determination that I knew was final.

I turned with a few curse words on my lips for dramatic affect and left.

The Skorniakoffs had many friends among the American military and I was just one of the enlisted men included in their group. I was scheduled to leave China in a few days according to rumors and would not see them again before I left. I assumed some of their more influential friends would be able to get Pop out of jail.

That night we got orders that we were shipping out the next day.

◆   ◆   ◆

The only person I could share all my concerns with was LaFoo and he really was not interested in them. He had driven the jeep for me when I delivered the lemons to Pop, but he did not enjoy sitting around with older people talking about history, civilian stories. He was not comfortable with my new friends and preferred the short time friends he made in the local bars which too often he would leave drunk and belligerent.

He considered my interest in learning to speak Chinese and having Chinese girl friend as a little odd just as he considered my interest in poetry.

I never introduced him to Aie Mei knowing that he hated the Asians and took any opportunity to bully them when he could.

When he walked along the sidewalk in the city he would walk straight ahead and make people in front of him move out of his way. Once an old man did not move fast enough and LaFoo grabbed him by the throat and pushed him into the gutter to my embarrassment. It was useless to talk to him. When he was drunk he would take more brutal pleasure in punching or kicking a civilian, or sailor, for no apparent reason. He tolerated only Marines, but not all of them either.

When I told him how badly I felt about not having time to say goodbye to my friends, he laughed. He had no remorse about leaving the people he had met in this part of the world.

The large transport ship called the USS Buckner nudged against the pier in Tsingtao on a gray, rainy morning in August 1946 as I and over thousands other Marines walked up her gangplanks. The busy streets and piers were not crowded and there were no rickshaw men pulling passengers as they were a little less than a year ago, when I arrived. In that short time, the mystery and romance of ancient China had become more familiar to me and I could identify people there I knew and loved. I looked with sadness as the land called China disappear from our moving transport which eased into the waters of the North China Sea, but glad that I was going home.

In a short time the six hundred foot, two funneled ship used her 20 knots speed to distance her from the land. Soon we were in deep water and the gray of the day turned by late afternoon into a wild storm. The bow and fan tail of the long ship began to alternately raise and sink into large swells that turned her into a child's toy. From the deck I could see the bow slice into the waves and sink so low I could touch the top of the water spray. In the distance we could see a small fishing boat which was caught in the storm and it was lifted high on a wave and then disappeared in a swell. Over and over the little boat rose and fell with the heaving waves. How could anyone be out here in such weather I wondered.

I went below with my thoughts of China, the sea, and the little Japanese fishing boat being tossed by the waves. I always wondered if the fishermen who were between China and Japan ever made it home.

In a few days we were in San Diego again where our journey began, and again there were no cheering girls and no bands. It seemed only yesterday that we waved goodbye to America, and at times never expected to return to, and now we had returned alive.

At Camp Pendleton we lined up before being assigned barracks, and a new group of Marines were training in the distance. There were hundreds of us standing in the parade ground when the sound of machine gun fire reached us. Immediately, hundreds of men fell to the ground to avoid the bullets they thought were coming their way. The machine gun firing was from the practice area, but still the reaction to hit the deck remained in our minds. The precaution learned in combat was still in our brain.

We picked ourselves off the deck sheepishly.

That night we saw for the first time the reason why we were home alive. A newsreel movie ran the explosion of the Atomic Bomb. I could not believe what I was seeing on the screen and wondered how I would have run from that one. The mushroom cloud was obscene, but saved our lives. What a terrible irony to contemplate.

A long train ride from the West Coast, across America over the Continental Divide past Salt Lake City and into Chicago brought us to the Great Lakes Naval Station in Illinois where we were formerly discharged after a physical and IQ test.

One of the noncoms asked me, "How would you like to stay in the Marines?"

"Not if you paid me a million dollars and made me a General," I said.

"You know," he said, "your IQ is 97."

At that time I did not know what that number meant but figured that 97 was not very good the way the guy sneered at me. But I did know that I did not want to remain.

Once a Marine was enough for me.

They gave LaFoo and me two tickets on the night train to New York and our pay. I had three hundred dollars.

LaFoo and I had seats facing a middle aged civilian couple who chatted to us more than we wanted to but they were very cordial and especially fond of Louie with his cherubic pink face and blue eyes. When among civilians we called LaFoo, Louie.

I remembered him sleeping peacefully next to me as the train rolled through the night. His baby face, pink and soft, with only a slight hint of a beard made him look cute. He looked like a little boy, and the woman kept smiling and looking at him with motherly appreciation.

Louie was still nineteen, and had been away from home a little over two years. I was a little older. Age wise, we were still just kids, but I kept thinking of our experiences. I remembered the civilian LaFoo had killed when the man asked to be shot. I remembered the bullet hole in his helmet, and the sound of approaching bombs that did not intimidate him. There was so much to remember that happened in such a short time.

Was this the same kid, sleeping peacefully with a little smile on his lips, and being admired by the nice lady and her husband? Was the brain in that body the same that controlled it so brutally not long ago? I wondered what the lady would say if I told her what LaFoo did during combat. I knew the young man she admired was not the same I had known. We were all so different below the surface that was apparent to the world. Our experiences had aged us internally while our faces still retained vestiges of our youth. It was a time to forget. We had lives to live that many others lost.

"He's such a sweet looking boy," she told her husband who smiled in agreement. And they were right, we were mostly sweet looking boys, and as our discharge papers said, our character was, 'Excellent'.

8

Heroes, Cowards, War

"War? What is it good for? Jerry Seinfeld, comedian.

"Dulce est Por Patria Mori." A World War I slogan denounced as "an old lie" by thousands of mothers and fathers who had lost their sons in war.

"You dirty, no good son of a bitch. You cowardly bastard. You're a disgrace to this army and you're going right back to the front to fight, although that's too good for you. You ought to be lined up against a wall and shot. In fact I should shoot you myself." General George Patton, speaking in an Army Hospital to a Private suffering combat fatigue.

I was home now. Perhaps my frightened prayers to God saved me, or was it the fact that I had broken down under stress? I chose the latter as the reason, and never felt comfortable about it. I always felt a little ashamed. I had saved my bag of skin by cracking up. No one seemed to care, but I knew how General Patton felt about us.

The wars continued almost immediately. I was attending college under the GI Bill of Rights. Otherwise, it would have been a job to the textile mills as a laborer. I got a notice from my draft board informing me that I was selected to serve in the Korean War. Immediately, I called to inform them that I had just been discharged and had served my time. The idea of possibly going back sent shivers through me. It turned out to be a bureaucratic error by the draft board that was still calling up men in my age group.

My kid brother, Jules, and my friend Billy, along with thousands of others were now old enough to be called, and they went to Korea. How could I warn them? I was only a year or two older than they and realized what they were headed for, but could not try to explain, just as my father, Tony, and father-in-law, Charlie, could not explain to me. I was a generation away from those two men who had fought in World WarII, but my brother and Billy were my contemporaries. The wars were coming too fast.

162

The Korean War killed and wounded thousands of Americans just a little younger than I, while I was in attending college. I felt like an old man among the college students whose fathers were paying the bills. I read with great empathy, about the Korean War, that cold, terrible, confused, and almost forgotten war that had no victory.

Then the Viet Nam war began, and lingered for years. I was married by then and had small children.

As I savored the happiness of life during the Viet Nam years, my personal demons faded and I said to myself, this is my time to enjoy what I had prayed for in the foxholes. That time, when I thought about all the older men sleeping with their wives and enjoying their families, while I and my buddies were about to be killed, was over. Now it was my time to enjoy life. Now I was the guy in a clean bed with his wife, ready to get up in the morning while other young men were in jungles dying.

I would get up soon, as I did those mornings, and check on my two young daughters who slept. A wonderful feeling of peace, contentment and love would fill my heart seeing them. It was so good to be alive. It was all that I had dreamed and prayed for.

Then, every morning in those dirty years of our history I would turn the radio on and listen to the latest casualty report. Each morning the numbers increased, reminding me that young kids were dying while I was enjoying the good life, while I was making love to my wife, while I was hugging my children, and while I was going to work and planning a future.

"The latest reports from the Defense Department released this morning indicates that one thousand, one hundred and fifty two names have been added to the American dead in Viet Nam this week." The commentator solemnly read.

Every morning the list was increased, until it reached to nearly forty thousand. The number of casualties were not reported anymore, the numbers were probably too high, or not news worthy. That was our morning wake up report in America those years, for so many years, the Viet Nam K.I.A. numbers. We listened to them at breakfast. I listened to the death numbers every morning as I drank my coffee, and told my wife I was ashamed for being so happy.

I knew what those numbers meant. I knew that those were young men torn apart and robbed of their future, robbed of making love, of having children, and watching their children grow. They were not just numbers. Those were shattered dreams and lives, not only of the men killed, but also the lives thousands of people who loved them. We were existing during a time of insane human sacrifice of young men by a government that did not have an acceptable reason, or a valid explanation.

We knew someone was lying to us as our boys were being killed, and being ordered to insanely kill and maim hundreds of thousands of native people.

I felt guilty, dirty, and hypocritical in those years, although glad to be alive. I had paid my dues, I told myself, but knowing the dues being paid by those boys saddened me.

Many Americans were looking for ways to have their sons avoid Viet Nam. This was not a war in which to die for your country. The wave of pain radiated from the victims of Viet Nam, and joined in the gigantic agony of all previous wars, and it continues.

I continued to enjoy life and got to be an old man. I have grandchildren now who are of the cannon fodder age.

Yesterday, I read that many young men are escaping to Canada to avoid service in the Iraqi war in progress just as many had done during the Viet Nam years. Canada is threatening to close its borders to American war objectors. I read that many of our boys are suffering combat stress in Iraq as the death list increases.

At the beginning of this war they ran the photos of those killed, on TV, as a bell tolled it the background, but now the list is too long. It would take too much valuable TV time, and probably bore the people anyway. If the death list increases enough they will build another monument.

Ask not for whom the bell tolls, it tolls for all of us.

And there is no end to it. Already in the planning, are more wars. We have a list of the evil nations who may harm us, and warn them that war may be the solution.

Since the Viet Nam years our country has developed into a super power without equal. Our weapons are so sophisticated and powerful that they overwhelm our enemies and our conflicts are almost one sided fights and, for the most part, short lived. The prolonged, intense combat conditions of past wars that psychologically crushed so many has changed, but still takes its toll. If combat exposure is increased, so will the psychological casualties.

Early in 1993, with more than 4,000 Gulf War veterans reporting symptoms of emotional instability, VA doctors were telling GIs that they were suffering from "psychological stress"—a phrase that as most in the Pentagon understood was considered by soldiers to be synonymous with "cowardliness".

In December 2004 an article appeared in the New York Times indicating that the country could expect tens of thousands of veterans from Iraq to flood our hospitals with emotional problems because of the war.

These results are surprising when you consider we are combating second and third rate powers. They do not match our military prowess, not to belittle the ordeal of those serving there, but our casualties will increase when the opposition strengthens.

A report by the Office of the United States Surgeon General was distributed during the World War ll explaining that the key to understanding the psychiatric problem is the simple fact that the danger of being killed or maimed imposes a strain so great that it causes men to break down.

There is "no such thing", the report continued, "as 'getting used to combat,' and it went on to explain that: 'Each man up there' knows that at any moment he may be killed, a fact kept constantly before his mind by the sight of dead and mutilate men around him. Each moment of combat imposes a strain so great that men will break down in direct relation to the intensity and duration of their exposure. Thus, psychiatric casualties are as inevitable as gunshot and shrapnel wounds."

During the World War II, over 1,393,000 were rejected for psychological reason that would make them ineffective in combat. Hundreds of thousands more were discharged for the same reasons after passing the indoctrination test, and being placed on active duty. Over 21,000 American military personnel were convicted of desertion, 49 were sentenced to death, but only one, Private Ernie Slovik, was executed.

During the current conflicts, several cases have been made against American soldiers who were accused of desertion, cowardice and similar charges. The determination of these charges has not been publicized, and certainly hasn't resulted in conviction and execution. The sad case of Private Slovik still remains as an anomaly.

Other nations have executed many of their military for similar charges, but under pressure from various groups when peace was declared, have offered to 'recover the lost honor' of those they killed. They tried to erase the stigma from the family names.

Eight years after the Great War, France sought to 'recover the honor' of the hundreds of soldiers who were executed for 'cowardice', Italy and Germany did the same. A generation of young men had been killed, and they wanted to let bygones be bygones and rectify a few errors.

The Russians and Japanese executed thousands of their own 'cowards' in the field. These were men who deserted or refused to fight. There are no exact records of how many. In those governments there were little records of anything, including the mistaken programs that took millions of lives for no purpose.

The simple fact is that man was not designed to endure war but has done so for centuries for many nebulous reasons. When required to protect family and friends I believe the most timid of us would stand and fight as best we could against the danger. We would not need slogans, or movies to motivate us if the cause was personal and just.

When the cause is abstract, disguised and warped, the reluctance to serve is more likely, and more understandable. In either case, a person is physically and mentally constructed with limited ability to endure stress, physically and mentally. In a just, and critical cause his efforts are still limited regardless of his passion. Given a reasonable alternative to war, without sacrificing a just position, most men and women would choose not to fight.

However, during any memorial gathering of veterans for any battle or war, large or small, where young men have died, you will hear the words recently expressed by an American President, "You all knew that some things are worth dying for. One's country is worth dying for, and democracy is worth dying for."

Dulce est Por Patria Mori, all over again.

Epilogue

The world was moving fast when we got home and I knew that my only chance for a better life was to take advantage of the GI Bill of Rights and get an education. This was an opportunity many of us would only have after going through the experiences I've written about here.

What we never had the money to buy, we purchased by placing ourselves within the reach of death, although the government saw it as a gift. In any case, it was wonderful.

LaFoo, after a try at civilian life decided that he missed the military and reenlisted. I saw him once during a brief visit he made to New Jersey. I was married then and a father. We had little to say to each other about current things, and those insane, cruel days we shared, embarrassed us, and were never discussed seriously. Only the events that were filled with fun and laughter, we relived.

One of the difficult adjustment JD had to make after the war was making love to his wife. He felt guilty about his missing leg until they finally began making a joke about it.

He had a hard time getting leverage to perform in bed. He had tried sleeping with a prosthesis and without. He asked Deirdre how she felt about it. She did not know, nor care. JD was the only guy she ever loved. They had children. He had to explain to his sons about his leg, adjusting the story for them to understand as they grew.

He had to defend his 'million dollar wound' for the rest of his life to the VA people during budget cuts when they tried to reduce his disability payments. He got a one hundred dollar discount from his real estate taxes and a special license plate that showed he was a disabled veteran and qualified for special parking privileges. And, oh yes, the Purple Heart.

The Boston Navy yard is still there and will be as long as there is a country called America. I took my children there for a visit when they were teenagers and we went aboard Old Ironsides. We climbed Bunker Hill and went to the Concord Bridge. I did not tell them about my brig time.

Parris Island still makes the news whenever a DI mistreats a Boot, or misjudges a situation and someone gets badly hurt. The gnats are still there, the endless parade grounds, DIs, and Boots playing war games. Many in the country don't like, or believe in the Marine Corps, but many more believe that the country cannot do without it.

On Guadalcanal, where the Lever Company returned to harvest coconuts, the Kinugawa Maru has rusted more and scavengers have torn pieces from her for scrap and souvenirs. Skin diving tours from Australia go to dive in the waters surrounding her. Soon there will only be a pile of coral and ghosts.

The Communist took over China and allowed the Nationalist government to escape to Taiwan where it abused the people natives and finally disappeared.

For many years it was impossible to communicate with my Chinese friends in Communist China. Then we got lost in our daily lives, and then, a lifetime passed away.

The Skorniakoffs were designated as displaced person along with millions of other people in the world following the war. They were relocated to the Philippines and then finally came to the United States. Julie married a sailor and they had three sons and lived with Mom and Pop in Seattle. We wrote to each other over the years and Mom and Pop visited me and my family in New Jersey. I introduced them to my wife and two daughters and we all went to the World's Fair in the 1960's.

Julie divorced her sailor husband, died of cancer and left her boys to be raised by her parents. Pop had a long life and then died. Mom wrote to tell me. In 1993 I visited Mom in a nursing home in Seattle. She was ill but still full of ideas and plans. She had notes for a book she wanted to write. We wrote periodically, and every Christmas, and then the letters stopped. She was in her nineties.

Okinawa continues in the news as a very important base for the United States. The places that were so important to die for have been bulldozed and rearranged. Occasionally, some Marine is in the news for raping one of the Okinawan girls and the natives demonstrate to have the Marines leave.

A few plaques were erected describing events during the fighting there. One especially, is very popular, it tells of the death of the 85 student nurses, killed by American troops. Many Japanese make a pilgrimage to see it.

In the years that followed, as I predicted, there were all sorts of reunions of Japanese and American veterans on Okinawa. They dedicated monuments, and promised to forgive and forget. I did not feel comfortable to be there, so I did not attend. I never had anything against the Japanese, and never had anything to forgive them for.

I never bought a Japanese car either, while many Americans, including veterans did. I just did not want to participate in the attitude that "war is war, and business is business" as defined by radio propaganda and commercials. The radio that was degrading the Japanese a few years ago was now selling their cars. It seemed hypocritical to me.

Marine veterans have made several returns to the old battleground especially at the anniversaries, twenty fifth, fiftieth, and then no more.

The sixtieth anniversary just passed as this book went to press. I did not see anything in the papers remembering the date.

The country still tries to remember Krup, Karnes and all the others who died, on Memorial Day, once a year. There are so many to remember, and more are included now almost every day. We who were there, and those who lost loved ones there, in all the wars, suffer a memorial day, every day of our lives.

End

The Book

America is attacked, and young boys, still in high school, hear the news over the radio on a Sunday afternoon. They believe it would never affect them, but soon the events of the war engulfs and transforms them.

The United States Marine Corps wanted these boys.

Enlist with them, train, guard, fight and die with them. The words grab you by the scruff of your neck, and sticks your nose into the mind shattering horrors of war. Learn how fear can rob you of your courage, and how it feels to be called a "coward".

You are there, as they fight, suffer, and cry for their mother as they die, or bargain with God for salvation, knowing it won't come. It is based on the author's personal experiences, but is an appraisal of wars faced by the frightened, common man, yesterday and today.

Read it. Some day it may save someone you love.

978-0-595-34866-4
0-595-34866-1

Printed in the United States
29476LVS00005B/403-408